GREGORY KESLER | AMY KATES

BRIDGING ORGANIZATION DESIGN AND PERFORMANCE

5 WAYS TO ACTIVATE A GLOBAL OPERATING MODEL

WILEY

Library of Congress Cataloging-in-Publication Data is Available:

ISBN 978-1-119-06-422-0 (hardback)
ISBN 978-1-119-06-449-7 (ePDF)
ISBN 978-1-119-06-432-9 (ePub)

Cover Design: Wiley
Cover Image: iStock.com/step2626

Printed in the United States of America
10 9 8 7 6 5 4 3 2 1

In memory of Jay Galbraith, whose contributions
to the field of organization design are
at the foundation of our work.

In honor of our dear friend Julia Law, whose courage
and energy inspired as we wrote this book.

CONTENTS

FOREWORD

Running a global business is hard. Technology and information management innovations have made us more productive, but have also increased the rate at which leaders must make decisions in order to meet rising customer expectations for quality, speed, and choice.

Business leaders and human resource professionals have a combined responsibility in any organization to create an environment in which talented, hard-working people at all levels can collaborate across boundaries to execute complex strategies. The core of this work is talent management and organization design and development.

CEOs and other top business leaders are becoming much more sophisticated about how to overcome the frustrations in making global-matrix organizations work effectively through management processes, collaborative governance, and selection and development of the right leadership talent. Getting these complex structures to work is a learning process for any large company managing multinational growth initiatives. CEOs and their top teams own this work in companies that are making the most progress. It is not delegated to staff managers or consultants.

The human resources function can provide business leaders with robust decision frameworks, performance analytics and insights, efficient and inclusive methodology, and ways to monitor and adjust plans as changes are implemented. Creating the right decision support for line managers is among the highest value activities for the HR function, just as it is for other functions. For example, a core premise of an effective decision science in areas such as finance, marketing, and operations is to provide frameworks that are consistent whether decisions are made at corporate, unit, or functional levels. Examples include "net present value," "customer segmentation," and "logistical optimization." Business units do not reinvent net present value or logistics optimization to suit their particular preferences. The HR function, however, has had few consistent and tested decision frameworks to offer managers in the realm of organization design.

In *Bridging Organization Design and Performance*, Greg Kesler and Amy Kates build off of the conceptual foundation laid by Jay Galbraith over the past 30 years to provide executives and HR professionals with exactly the decision tools needed to bring sophisticated global organizations to life. In this book, they introduce the concept of *activation*, which goes beyond implementation. Activation is the dynamic, multiyear journey of analysis, design, evaluation, and adjustment of the organizational "wiring" needed to make strategic intent a reality.

Kesler and Kates provide a rich narrative on the successes and the misses of many global companies to help readers create their own road map for activation. You will find that this book speaks to the questions that many CEOs and CHROs want answers to:

- How do I match my organization to our growth strategies without creating undue complexity?

- How do I harness the energy of global networks for innovation and speed while leveraging the diverse assets of the organization?

- How do I ensure the right planning, decision-making, and performance evaluation conversations are occurring across geographic, product, and functional boundaries and set them up for success?

- What type of talent thrives in complex, global environments, and how do I build a pipeline of leaders able and willing to work in a matrix?

- What is the practical plan for assessing and adjusting as we go?

With this book, Kesler and Kates make a significant contribution to the decision science behind organization design and development. Business leaders and HR professionals will find it a practical guide for gaining competitive advantage from their global organization.

John Boudreau
Professor, Management & Organization, Marshall School of Business
Research Director, Center for Effective Organizations
University of Southern California, Los Angeles

CHAPTER 1

The Global Operating Model

A FAILURE OF STRATEGY OR EXECUTION?

Companies that compete globally must have sophisticated playbooks for sustaining competitive advantage in the face of myriad new challengers, continued waves of technological change, and uncertain economic and regulatory environments. As a result, leaders of these companies must design organizations capable of immense creativity and agility to manage the tension that is inherent in complex, global strategies.

The economic recovery of 2010–2015 has triggered a number of high-profile mergers, but even more breakups and spinoffs among large global companies, particularly those based in the United States. Between 2012 and 2014 alone, Kraft, Royal Philips, Hewlett Packard, Ingersoll Rand, ConocoPhillips, Darden, and eBay agreed to split off substantial portions of their businesses in response to a groundswell of hostility toward underperforming diversified companies. The chief executives of iconic companies including DuPont, Amgen, and GE were under pressure from activist investors such as Bill Ackman, Nelson Peltz, Daniel Loeb, and Carl Icahn to do the same. Even Procter & Gamble announced its intention to shed more than 50 percent of its brands "in order to simplify the way we organize and manage the company" (Byron 2014).

As organization designers, this trend intrigues us. Have conglomerates and diversified companies underperformed because of failures in enterprise strategy? Or are these companies failing the acid test for organization effectiveness, stumbling on execution brought about by lumbering, layered, and siloed organizational models unsuited to delivering on diverse, global strategies? Hewlett Packard's CEO, Meg

Whitman, defended plans to break up the company into two parts. "Our markets are moving at lightning speed, both the enterprise market as well as the printing and PC market, and we need to be faster, we need to be more nimble, we need to have a cost structure that is appropriate for the competitors that we face in both those businesses," she told the business press in May 2015 (CNBC 2015). Cost increases of about $400 million are expected to be offset by other synergies in the two separate companies at the end of 2017.

THE GLOBAL OPERATING MODEL

The global operating model is the means to manage this complexity, this tension, this need for both leverage and agility. It is the artful combination of organizational structure, process, governance forums, metrics, and reward systems that tie together global business units and functions with far-flung geographic market units. The global operating model is intended to structure interactions at the strategic nodes that will build and execute needed capabilities. Global operating models are typically composed of three dimensions:

1. Geographic market units (regions, countries, or country clusters)

2. Global business units (products, brands, categories, or customer segments)

3. Global operating and support functions (R&D, supply chain, marketing, IT, HR, finance, etc.)

Figure 1.1 illustrates how Deere & Co. defines the relationship among its region–market units, global product platforms, and worldwide functions.

In addition to Deere, companies such as Nike, P&G, Medtronic, PepsiCo, Unilever, IBM, Levi Strauss, and Philips have created elegant organization models and consider their worldwide, matrix organizations to be sources of competitive advantage. Some leadership teams inhabit these models as though they are second nature. Others struggle mightily.

No companies have completely solved the challenges of bringing these complex organizational models to life, but many have made great

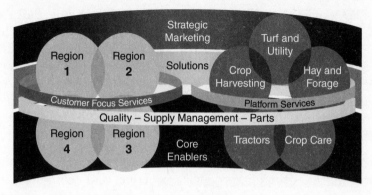

Figure 1.1 Deere's global operating model.
Source: Deere & Co.

progress. Studying these companies up close is productive. There are reasons some deliver superior results with these organizational arrangements while others seem to have real problems. This book will explore what factors yield success and provide a road map to effectiveness that any leadership team can follow.

GLOBAL OPERATING MODEL

An interdependent set of organization structures, processes, governance, metrics, and reward systems that tie together center-based business and functional teams and diverse geographic teams in order to execute complex strategies around the world.

WHY ORGANIZATION IS AS IMPORTANT AS STRATEGY

Profitable growth comes not from the articulated strategy, but a company's actual strategy, which is reflected in how the organization's resources are allocated. Outdated capabilities, structures, and decision-making processes get in the way of implementing good intentions and block attention for new sources of growth. In effect, the backward pull of structure, if left unattended, inhibits the very best laid strategic plans.

CEOs of large multinational companies can overcome the central challenge of designing for growth by building critical organizational capabilities that build the bridge from strategy to structure to performance. Such enterprisewide capabilities are difficult to build. They are cultivated by the intentional arrangement of structure, process, metrics, and talent. Organizational capabilities are a distinct source of competitive advantage that enable both the rapid execution of strategy and the envisioning of new strategic options.

Most of the truly critical capabilities that drive growth—innovation, brand building, digital marketing, and ecommerce—are formed at the intersections of business units, functions, and geographic markets as shown in Figure 1.2 below.

For example, after years of failed attempts to penetrate Asian and Latin American markets with its best-in-class agricultural equipment, Deere & Co. embraced the reality that retrofitting its American product lines (tractors, planters, harvesters, etc.) for emerging markets was not the solution for competing against tough local players that could bring low-cost equipment to farmers with good-enough levels of reliability. "Shifting the center of gravity" from Moline, Illinois to Pune, India helped bring a very different mindset to product development in emerging markets (Govindarajan and Trimble 2012). However, it would be years before Deere could overcome the immense regulatory barriers in China in order to provide cheap capital to small farmers who, instead, chose to buy low-cost Chinese tractors and planters. Meanwhile, Deere's investment in state-of-the-art paint

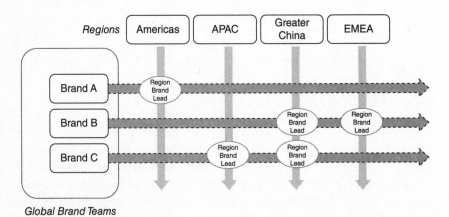

Figure 1.2 **Growth comes at the intersection of global and local.**

systems in China and its global rollout of sophisticated production process and engineering standards appeared to its critics as grossly overengineered for markets with price points that simply could not support those levels of process innovation. Deere's new global operating model, implemented in 2009, is intended to more nimbly manage the tensions among developed and developing markets across its five product platforms.

Or consider Nike, marketing a core brand across a number of consumer categories with hundreds of footwear and apparel products all over the world. The voice of the global soccer consumer has made its way into Nike's day-to-day decision making, and with record-setting results. But the seasonal marketing story line for the *swoosh* has to work for basketball, running, fitness, and other consumer categories too, so the global soccer team has to line up behind a bigger marketing idea. That's only the beginning of the creative conflict. South Africa might want to go one way on footwear design profiles and color palettes while the Netherlands, South Korea, and Brazil have other ideas. And apparel, footwear, and accessories have to fit together as an integrated collection for the footballer in all of those markets.

To ignore any of these competing voices diminishes the potential of Nike's powerful blend of brand, design, and market reach. It must be agile, but it must leverage its design prowess and its considerable cost structure. Nike executives cannot afford to keep things simple and make the wrong compromises. Nike's top team is very deliberate about how to work the complexity and the tension across the matrix in their organization to competitive advantage.

Both of these examples illustrate how sophisticated management of the connections and conversations across product lines, markets, and functions are needed to drive growth strategies.

AGILITY VERSUS LEVERAGE

The global operating model, with its multiple dimensions, embodies the promise of the matrix organization—that a company can have it all: robust global products and brands, local market responsiveness, and cost-effective functional processes and systems. The reality is that many senior executives in companies trying to execute global strategy are frustrated by the challenges of meeting *any* of these objectives.

Mike Canning, CEO of Duke Corporate Education, observes: "In the past, many organizations moved to a matrix to better position themselves for opportunities and customer solutions; decades later, they are still trying to figure out why it isn't working. CEOs discuss how their companies have 'perfected the art of working in silos.' Leaders point out that collaboration across business units remains challenging because people are not properly incentivized and no single business unit will bear the burden of investing in collaboration" (Canning 2015).

Efforts to get closer to the customer through stronger regionally based commercial organizations do not necessarily lead to greater customer focus. In fact, strong regional autonomy can slow the movement of brand-building ideas across regions and lead to duplication of programs, addition of redundant resources, and shadow functions springing up in distant corners of the business. Smaller, autonomous business units also slow the movement of talent and other resources to new growth targets, trapping resources in slower-growth priorities (Sull, Homkes, and Sull 2015). Then, when the central groups attempt to exert control, decision making often grinds to a crawl and leaders can feel they are living in a house of mirrors.

Underlying these difficulties are two opposing objectives continuously in play in the global operating model: agility and leverage. *Agility* delivers speed and flexibility—the ability to anticipate and respond to opportunities quickly. *Leverage* is the advantage conferred by size—influence with suppliers and distributors, the ability to invest in technology, systems, and talent with less overall cost than what the operating units could accomplish on their own. All too often the more a company tries to realize the benefits of leverage by imposing common ways of work from the center, the slower and less agile that decision making out in the markets tends to become. But it doesn't have to be this way.

Smart leaders move toward a balance in decision authority between the global and local elements of their organizations as shown in Figure 1.3. PepsiCo's CEO, Indra Nooyi, is skillfully realigning decision authority for brand building and product creation away from decades of local business management to more center-led, cross-regional, and cross-category decision making. In contrast, executives of companies that have long operated with heavyweight global business units, like Royal Philips, are rebuilding skills, capability,

Figure 1.3 Balancing power in the matrix is rarely a once-and-done task.

and governing authority back into regional markets, especially in developing countries. Strong market leader positions have been added to 11 of Philips' critical growth markets. The market leader roles work across the 20 or so business units, at the local level, to maximize the company's influence with regulatory agencies, suppliers, sources of talent, and distribution-channel partners. Instead of trying to sell globally standardized products around the world, Philips develops locally relevant offerings. As an example, shaving products are designed to fit the specific facial hair needs of different regions. "We are not shipping the same devices worldwide; our products reflect the specific needs of each market," says Jeroen Tas, top executive of Philips Healthcare Informatics Solutions and Services. But Philips CEO Frans van Houten makes the case for balancing this agility with leverage. "I cannot allow hundreds of product managers to go their own way. It is unrewarded complexity when everybody invents their own process, as it hampers cross-learning and efficiency" (Mocker et al. 2014).

Managers tend to associate agility with small, focused, and highly autonomous local units that can move quickly. This is certainly true from the local perspective. But, many local profit and loss (P&L) units

Table 1.1   Two different kinds of agility.

When Decentralized Business Units Add Agility	When Being More Center-Led Adds Agility (Enterprise)
• Local business units adapt the offering to local tastes and preferences	• Top executives make hard, objective choices about getting in and out of businesses
• Product innovation can move quickly in focused business units	• Resources and talent can be shifted across business lines and initiatives quickly
• Business units know their competitors and can react quickly to challenges	• Technologies and information can move across segments
	• Companywide view of innovation opportunities leads to bigger ideas

actually limit agility at the enterprise level. The company is less able to flexibly use resources and shift focus to new growth spaces (Sull 2009). Consider Apple's very large, functional organization model with its single P&L at the top. Apple has proven to be a far more agile organization than Microsoft, with its entrenched product division structure, in terms of ability to anticipate and respond to the arrival of cloud-based computing and smartphones as an Internet platform. Apple's organization also ensures that the consumer experience is the same across all products and applications. At the same time, Apple achieves remarkable degrees of leverage with its scale and the outsized popularity of its centrally led brand. Table 1.1 summarizes the different types of agility that can be achieved.

THE CHALLENGE OF ACTIVATION

There are only so many ways to design enterprise structure. The gravitational pull to greater complexity, and all the challenges that come with it, is powered by the need for new sources of growth in diverse geographic markets across multiproduct divisions with increasingly demanding customers and consumers with lots of technology at their fingertips (Galbraith 2009). After working closely with over 25 large

US and European-based global companies during the past seven years, we have concluded the problem is not in the fundamental design of these operating models. The challenge is ineffective and incomplete *activation*. Despite large-scale, well-funded change initiatives, sophisticated communication programs, and countless worldwide leadership summits, the hard work of bringing these complex organization designs to life often lacks focus or is not sustained over the three or more years that it typically takes to fully embed new ways of working.

As we look across the companies we have studied and worked with, we see a common set of symptoms that indicate incomplete activation:

• Excess layers and duplicated work make the organization slow and internally focused. Over time mid- to large-cap companies tend to build in layers of organization. Overreliance on structure and hierarchy to coordinate and control work not only adds cost, but also makes organizations slow and internally focused. Collaboration (both internal and external) is easier with fewer organizational levels, where each level plays a unique and value-adding role. While hierarchy is likely to continue to play a role in future organization models, it must be simplified, and more emphasis placed on horizontal connections.

• Global product teams and functions are overlaid onto the existing regional (commercial) organizations without adjustments in legacy P&L structures, creating unproductive friction. Companies do not become more global just because they have added worldwide product and brand teams, or global functions and councils, to manage centrally driven growth strategies and programs. Rather, companies become truly global when they have carefully orchestrated relationships among global, regional, and local teams with strong, interactive partnerships. The business targets and processes they comanage, and the nature of talent that staff these new roles, are all part of bringing global organization to life. Many companies eager to implement a new organizational structure simply do not have the wisdom, patience, and discipline to change the larger system. Too often, new initiatives and P&L structures are layered in without redesign of the larger whole.

• Power dynamics remain unresolved across global business units, regional teams, and functional units. Power for purpose should define how decisions will be made in the connections between global businesses, global functions, and regional or local businesses. The design of a global operating model is not complete until these decision-making ground rules and forums are defined, and too many executive teams leave this guidance to chance or to the political forces that unfold among strong personalities in the company. Having said that, some companies believe decision rights can be simply spelled out in detail with RACI (Responsibility, Accountability, Consult, Inform) charts and the like. This is also a fallacy.

• Global functions are designed to do yesterday's work, often independently from the needs of the business (and businesses have low expectations for functions). No one knows for sure where the future of management is headed, but it's clear that management teams must adapt to new ways of working, enabled by continuous waves of technology. The work of support and operating functions like finance, marketing, supply chain, and human resources must change to leverage these technologies, and do so in a way that serves enterprise objectives as well as the needs of individual businesses.

• Leaders do not know how and are not motivated to work in a matrix—metrics and reward systems continue to reinforce lack of enterprise thinking. Uncertainty is unnerving for most of us. Big organizations have been designed to eliminate uncertainty, and generations of leaders have been trained to allocate resources where assets are certain to produce the greatest return. "Silo thinking" is a rational response to the definition of success. But leaders who succeed in the global operating model demonstrate high degrees of learning agility, challenge existing business models, and colead growth strategies with partners in other parts of the world. They have grown up moving through jobs that take them across regions, cultures, functions, and business models. As importantly, the metrics and reward systems in the company make it clear that this kind of collaboration is expected.

• The corporate executive committee continues to act as a group of individual leaders, each focused entirely on their own business versus the needs of the enterprise. The top executive teams in successful global companies spend time together, sharing the enterprise leadership role. When the sole focus of top leaders is on their own business results, the message is clear to those who look up to them, and subtle or not-so-subtle forms of internal competition prevail. This is an often-ignored element in activating the new organization.

In short, it's one thing to design global business units, regional operating units, and worldwide functions; it's quite another to figure out how to get them to interact effectively to serve consumers and customers profitably.

If you are with a fast-growing, successful company and you have read this far, you may be feeling that this book doesn't apply to you. Or maybe you are wondering how these concepts apply to the technology industry. Haven't the likes of Google shown that culture trumps organization? How do these learnings from mature, and sometimes sclerotic, companies apply to the twenty-first century organization? Why are we talking about layers and processes and power dynamics—isn't hierarchy going to be replaced with holocracy? We would point out that nearly all companies have a phase where high growth, a strong founding culture, and robust revenues or profits make worrying about organization design a rather esoteric concern. This phase can last years or decades. However, leaders easily become imprisoned by their past successes (Govindarajan and Trimble 2012). The "dominant logic"—which forms the very culture that led to past success and which is deeply held and shared across the organization and implanted in the minds of leaders, their relationships, and the way they plan, organize work, make decisions, and evaluate and reward people—becomes a barrier. One only has to look at the airline, car, publishing, media, or telecommunications industries to find plenty of examples of previously successful companies caught flat-footed when disruptive competitors came on the scene with new business models.

This book is for leaders of companies that need to activate a new global operating model in response to external change as well as those who are looking for insight into how to design the global organization to create the most value and unlock growth and performance that will win in the marketplace. It is also for forward-looking leaders of companies that are on a high-growth trajectory, but want to avoid being surprised to find themselves one day unprepared when a new formula for success is required.

OUR RESEARCH

Throughout the book we will draw upon our organization design and activation work with 25 global, matrixed companies across industries as well as some nonprofits. The companies range in size from about $3 billion to $65 billion. We also tap into research on other companies, utilizing the work of other writers and public accounts in the media.

The danger of featuring any company in a business book is that today's shining example can stumble or be eclipsed in just a few years' time, making the book feel dated. All of the companies cited in this book are doing many things right. They have leadership actively engaged in creating organizations that meet the needs of their customers, employees, communities, and shareholders. All have developed and adopted best practices that can benefit your company. None, however, are complete, and that is not a failing. Running a global company is a complex endeavor. As consultants we admire the dedication and inspiration that we see front-line employees, managers, and leaders bring to their work. We thank the many companies and leaders that we have had the privilege of working with. Our goal here is to share what we have learned.

ORGANIZATION OF THE BOOK

The book is organized into 11 chapters.

- Chapter 2 explores the rewards and the challenges of global operating models.

- Chapter 3 defines *activation* and provides examples of what effective and ineffective activation looks like.

- Chapters 4–8 present each of the five activators in detail: anchor layer, networks, business handshake, decision making, and matrix-ready leaders.

- Chapter 9 discusses the design process for activation and will be of particular interest to organization development and human resource professionals.

- Chapter 10 provides a summary view across the five activators, and highlights a number of ways that they interact to bring new organization models to life.

- Chapter 11 contains a health check to get you started on assessing your organization and focusing your activation work. It includes a set of tools organized by the five activators.

SUMMARY OF THE CHAPTER

- Organization design delivers strategy execution by building capabilities that matter.

- Most of the critical growth capabilities are found in the intersections of global and local businesses and functions where innovation, customer care, consumer intimacy, and brand building happen.

- Tension in the matrix is there for a reason. Competing voices in the matrix organization are sources of value for shareholders and customers. Healthy tension is how you exploit the many assets of a big company.

- Most global operating models are built around three dimensions: global business line, regional market units, and global functions.

- Agility and leverage are equally important to big companies, and the organization design must deliver both.

- Since most global operating structures are designed around the same three dimensions, the real differentiator is activation. Most companies don't fully activate their global operating models.

CHAPTER 2

Sources of Complexity

Complex organizations are a result of complex business strategies. But not all complexity is equal. Frans van Houten, CEO of Royal Philips, makes a case for distinguishing between what he calls *rewarded* and *unrewarded complexity*. *Rewarded* complexity drives a multifaceted growth strategy through a network of value-adding contact points across diverse teams, functions, and business units around the world. A well-designed organization structure brings management attention to the nodes where value and capabilities are created—the intersection of customers, brands, products, emerging markets, functional expertise, and other strategic choices.

Often, rewarded complexity is a result of making things simpler or more compelling for customers. The powerful Walmart business units inside P&G, Unilever, and other consumer brand companies create enormous complexity challenges for the leadership of these companies, but Walmart, the customer, is well served by this single point of interface. This is a value-creating form of tension. Conversely, when organization models are made "simple" for leaders to manage internally, the customer is often left to navigate the supplier's inner workings or to interact with multiple sales representatives across different product divisions. The complexity is pushed out to the customer.

Unrewarded complexity is largely the result of unnecessary layering and misalignments among structure, roles, decision rights, processes, and rewards systems. Confusion and frustration, internally and for customers, are nearly always symptoms of organizations that have fuzzy roles and decision rights, competing incentive systems, and leaders who do a poor job managing across boundaries. It is this unrewarded complexity that has made matrix organization structures lightning rods. Managers and employees blame the organizational model, when in fact it is poor activation that is to blame for unwieldy,

Table 2.1   Rewarded and unrewarded complexity.

Rewarded Complexity	Unrewarded Complexity
Reflects the complexity of the strategy—the number of *connection points* among business units and functions necessary to extract the most value from a company's many assets.	Unnecessary layers, P&L units, dual reporting, and duplication combined with ineffective management and business processes and metrics are the recipe for unrewarded complexity.

conflicting ways of working. The difference between rewarded and unrewarded complexity is summarized in Table 2.1.

Strategic complexity can yield competitive advantage, but only if the organization is designed to extract the rewards. There is no reason for leaders to avoid complex strategies. However, if such strategic paths are chosen, understand the predictable implications and make design choices that maximize rewarded complexity and minimize unrewarded complexity.

Strategic choices create three kinds of organization complexity as shown in Table 2.2. The categories of strategic choices and the type of complexity they lead to are:

1.   Global/local (challenges of coordinating across geography)

2.   Business portfolio (challenges of finding synergies across substrategies)

3.   Horizons for growth (challenges of focusing management attention on different timeframes)

Table 2.2   How strategy choices drive organizational complexity.

	Less Organizational Complexity		More Organizational Complexity
Global/Local Businesses	Local for local	Global, delivered locally	Mix of global and local
Portfolio Complexity	Domestic company or holding company	Loosely related divisional units	Closely related divisional units
Nature of Strategy Horizons	Horizon 1 primarily	Horizons 1 and 2	Horizons 1, 2, and 3

GLOBAL/LOCAL: THE MANY FACES OF GLOBAL COMPANIES

The path to global business management has not been a straight line. In the 1990s and the earliest years of this millennium, all bets called for a flatter world with movement toward more global products and more commonality in consumer tastes and go-to market practices. While some of this has turned out to be true, that picture is far too simple. In fact, consumer tastes remain stubbornly local, particularly in food, beverage, apparel, and other consumer goods. In business-to-business industries, equipment companies such as John Deere or medical devices companies like Medtronic cannot compete in India or China by retrofitting products engineered for developed markets, regardless of the reliability benefits these products may have over local competitors. Further, the European Union has hardly evolved into a single market, and developing markets have proven to be very difficult places to do business, with continued trade barriers and regulatory variations that add to the logistical challenges of moving goods and services across hobbled infrastructure.

Many companies are really a mix of both global and local brands and products. For years we watched the shrinking role of the country manager and the concurrent rise in authority of global product units in B2B and B2C companies alike. Today many companies are reallocating decision authority back to regions, particularly for developing countries that demand locally tailored products that can compete against emerging market players.

Consider the continuum of multinational companies in Figure 2.1. At the right end of the spectrum Philips and BMW market true global

LOCAL   GLOBAL

Local businesses are run as "local for local" within a market or country. There is no significant global added value business role.

Global-local businesses are run as a combination between global business platforms and local market business realization. These businesses require the *strongest connection between the global units and regional units.*

Global businesses can operate more simply from the center and depend less on the business market matrix.

Figure 2.1   Most global companies represent a mix of local/global assets.

products. Others, such as Nestlé, operate quite locally in most categories. A third group, and these drive the most organizational complexity, fall in the middle, with portfolios of both global and local products.

Heineken is a good example of a company with a broad and mixed portfolio of global and local brands as shown in Figure 2.2. Some, such as the Heineken brand, are global brands and are managed with a fairly heavy hand from Amsterdam in order to create a common brand message and position in the marketplace. Aspiring multinational brands such as Stella and Sol sit somewhere in between the Heineken brand and the local brews that are very popular in their regions and countries.

The global operating model must accommodate these variations. At GE Healthcare, innovations in electronic imaging devices for Asia are not devolved versions of their American counterparts, but entirely new designs suited to often radically different health care delivery infrastructure, sometimes performed in people's homes. Advertising and media themes at Coca-Cola for popular music and sports must be adapted to cultural variations in the Middle East and South Africa. Despite these differences among diverse markets, new product and brand-building ideas must travel and they must be commercialized quickly. Resources must be shared and leveraged to take advantage of the scale that smaller, local operators cannot match.

A business with a product offering that is either fully global or fully local can have fairly simple organizational arrangements. Power will be vested with global product groups for the former and geographic units for the latter. Strategies that employ a mix of global

Figure 2.2   Heineken's brands range from truly global to quite local.

and local products, or global products that must be highly adapted for local contexts, will require leaders to spend a lot of time managing the tension between product and market managers.

Business Portfolio Relatedness

A second type of strategic complexity has to do with the relationship among the various units in the business portfolio. A continuum of relationship is shown in Table 2.3.

The holding company, on the right of the continuum, is the least complex strategy in terms of organizational implications. Little synergy is expected or desired across operating units in the portfolio. However, some are like Danaher, known for its very lean corporate center and hands-off approach managing diverse divisions, which finds value across the portfolio through its superior ability to target and integrate acquisitions and then introduce the Danaher Business System of continuous improvement to run them efficiently.

At the other end, on the left, a single business is characterized by one primary business model. This model can be deployed across multiple brands and through operations in many geographies, as Coca-Cola and Marriott do, but there is only one full business unit. Such companies typically are characterized by two-dimensional functional/geographic matrix structures.

The most complex strategies—and hence the biggest challenge from an organization design and activation perspective—fall in the middle. A company that chooses to have multiple product lines or businesses with some relationship must add value over and above the individual contribution of the businesses as standalone companies. Otherwise, they are at a disadvantage to single business and holding company competitors.

Synergies can be realized in different ways (Galbraith 2014). Companies such as IBM actively seek to marry *solutions* for customers by combining products and services across operating units. Others seek *synergies* among business units by sharing intellectual property across the portfolio. For example, when Disney creates a character, it shows up in films, merchandising, park rides, and music and books; all separate business units. PepsiCo's snacks and beverages divisions share common customers and channels. Although innovation and

Table 2.3   Four types of companies in terms of portfolio integration (with some organizational indicators).

	Fully Integrated (Single Business)	Divisional (Closely Related)	Hybrid (Loosely Related)	Holding Company (Conglomerate)
Strategy & Organization Design	Single strategy guides all P&L units with minor variations	Complementary business portfolio and core strategies with synergies	Diverse, relatively autonomous businesses with limited synergies	Structuring cheap finance, buying and selling separate assets
Governance	Direction comes from organizational center All process and practices are common Single culture	Controlling certain key functions to drive scale, common process, and policy consistency Often matrixed front and back ops	Facilitating some scale benefits and some best practices across otherwise standalone businesses' capital, talent, and knowledge	Appointing the best people to run the businesses Business units return financials to parent No common processes Multiple cultures
Leadership Talent	Single talent pool for leadership jobs Numerous synergies expected	High degrees of cross-business unit movement of key talent with common process and metrics	Limited planned movement of talent across units at senior levels	No movement of talent across units No synergies expected
Rewards Philosophy	Single design, limited need for variations Central administration	Single design, with variations in practices as necessary Mixed administration	Harmonized variations in design with business unit administration	High variability; no need for harmonization
Company Examples	Apple, Cisco, Coca-Cola, Toyota,	P&G, IBM, Unilever Danone, PepsiCo	GE, PepsiCo, Philips, Johnson & Johnson	Berkshire Hathaway, Private Equity

manufacturing processes are quite different across the portfolio, PepsiCo's "power of one" organization model is creating a common go-to-market approach that leverages customer relationships and the company's extensive footprint.

Another way to create synergy across the portfolio is through shared technologies. Honeywell has delivered superior results under CEO Dave Cote, driving synergies across the automotive and aerospace businesses by exploiting the science and technology common to both businesses—aerodynamics, rotor dynamics, and materials. This transfer of knowledge has delivered benchmark know-how in power, torque, fuel efficiency, and emissions reduction, all critical to automotive producers. "Born out of our aerospace business, the automotive turbocharger is a miniature jet engine," Cote said in a statement announcing a 2014 organization change, adding that the realignment would further "leverage shared strengths and synergies" ("Honeywell Merging Turbocharger Business into Aerospace Unit" 2014).

Many pharmaceutical companies have both prescription and over-the-counter divisions in what would seem to be a closely related portfolio. The reality is that the business dynamics, regulatory environments, product innovation cycle times, and channels are completely different for prescription and consumer healthcare products. GlaxoSmithKline (GSK) is working hard to deliberately create connections across its portfolio through shared science. GSK's Steifel branded skin creams would have little advantage in a crowded consumer health care marketplace without the crossover to the prescription products. This Rx/Cx strategy requires organizational connections between product development and marketing if it is to result in a seamless product set in both the consumer and physician's mind.

A final way to create synergy is through shared infrastructure. Cargill is the largest privately held company based in the United States at $135 billion in revenue. It has a broad portfolio of nearly 70 business units organized into six global platforms. The businesses are all related in some way to food production, but represent an extremely diverse set of business models. Cargill runs hog and chicken processing plants, sells seed, fertilizer, and animal feed to farmers, mines salt for deicing roads, charters oceangoing transport ships, and sells risk management financial products to food producers. Customers are very different as are the capabilities, investments, and speed of business across a portfolio that spans manufacturing to hedge funds. However, Cargill has set up Cargill Business Services (CBS) to provide shared infrastructure across the platforms. CBS provides regionally based back-office transaction, data, and information management services that are common across employee groups and business processes. This shared foundation leverages the size of Cargill and frees up staff in finance, IT, human resources, and other functions to focus on creating the specific solutions that each business unit needs to compete in its unique niche. In this way, although Cargill has a fairly loosely related business portfolio, company leaders can find ways to leverage size and scale. Of course, negotiating what work and processes are common and which must be unique across the portfolio creates functional/business unit complexity that becomes the hard work of leadership.

HORIZONS FOR GROWTH

A third type of strategic complexity is driven by growth choices that need to be executed over differing time horizons. McKinsey's three horizon model is a useful way to illustrate strategic choices made in the dimension of time, as shown in Figure 2.3 (Baghai, Coley, and White 1999). Once established, all companies need to operate in Horizon 1—defending and extending the core business through product line extensions, marketing efforts, and process efficiencies. Most companies soon need to think about Horizon 2, which is typically focused

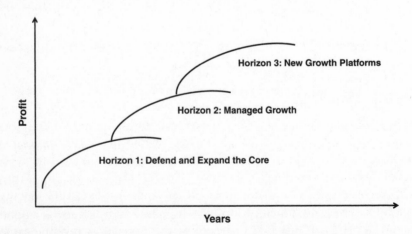

Figure 2.3   Growth horizons strategy map draws attention to three time frames for investment (Baghai, Coley, and White 1999).

on creating new products for existing customer segments or adapting the current success formula for new customer groups or markets. Horizon 2 activities usually generate less revenue in the short term than Horizon 1 investments and thus set up tension and conflict for resources between managers that have accountability for each.

True growth companies also operate in Horizon 3. Activities in this horizon often have quite uncertain payoff. These new growth platforms may even cannibalize Horizon 1 and 2 businesses, yet they have to be invested in as they often represent the key to sustainability. Consider a company such as Campbell's. Its Horizon 1 core business is canned soups and related simple meals and beverages, a category with limited growth potential as consumers turn to fresh convenience foods, but bolstered by the equity behind the iconic Campbell's brand. Growing the cracker, biscuit, and snack categories globally, represented by brands such as Pepperidge Farm, Australia's Arnott, and Denmark's Kelsen is a classic Horizon 2 set of strategies—expanding established success formulas into new markets. Full-force future growth, however, is represented by acquisitions such as Bolthouse Farms, Plum organics baby food, and local deli and dairy products. These new categories set the stage for a Horizon 3 health and wellness platform. These products reach different consumers, require different marketing, and even compete with core products. The strategy is smart; it allows Campbell's to compete on its current strengths while developing new capabilities. Successful execution across all three horizons, however, will test the capability of Campbell's leadership teams to allocate investments and management time and attention correctly across the portfolio.

STRATEGIC COMPLEXITY—TV MULTICHANNEL RETAIL EXAMPLE

QVC provides an example of how these three types of strategic complexity play out. Founded in 1986, the video and ecommerce retailer is a leader in creating communities of loyal customers through its uncanny ability to select and merchandise products that appeal to its core demographic—women, ages 35–65, with disposable income who like to buy good quality and contemporary merchandise at a good value. As of 2014, nearly 70 percent of the company's revenue came from the United States, with the rest from QVC operations in the U.K., Italy, Germany, Japan, and a joint venture in China. Customers who wish to buy products from QVC either phone a call center or go to the QVC.com website or mobile app to place an order. QVC is ranked as the sixth largest ecommerce player among multi-category retailers, and number 15 across all industries, according to the 2015 Internet Retailer Top 500 list.

The QVC growth strategy can be viewed through the three lenses discussed above, and these lenses can predict where the leadership team needs to focus in order to ensure that their strategic choices yield competitive advantage rather than unrewarded organizational complexity.

Global/Local. With a leading position in the US market, a core part of QVC's growth strategy is to bring its winning formula to new markets. The business requires a strong merchandising team in the field to understand local tastes, build vendor relationships, and be highly in tune with the customer and local competitors. For a business that operates live 24 hours a day nearly every day of the year and sells a breadth of product across multiple categories in each market, local operators need to be able to make decisions fast. Yet behind the product assortment and marketing decisions are many opportunities to create common process and infrastructure not just to save cost but also to share expertise and knowledge. QVC looks like a very local business, but is going to win against competitors by leveraging global merchandising, technology, and supply chain capabilities.

Portfolio Relatedness. Today, QVC is a single business model but may diversify its customer base to target broader demographics or to create partnerships that deliver the product and brand through new channels. These changes will create new interfaces and complexity in preserving the unique QVC brand experience across all touch points.

Horizon. Horizon 3 for QVC would be to deliver a completely digital experience that stands apart from the live broadcast. Even though QVC.com and the mobile app are quite robust, and customers do shop QVC independently from the broadcast, a majority of users go to the site or mobile app after watching the television broadcast. The next step is to build an interactive experience that attracts more new customers directly to digital platforms. The challenge will be to manage the inevitable competition with the core business, which still has a lot of growth potential.

■ ■ ■

If you want a simple organization, then pursue a simple strategy. Stay in one geography, with one business model, and find a product or service with few competitors. But if your growth strategy demands complexity, understand the organizational implications, primarily the tensions at strategic intersections. If you embrace these tensions and help the people in your organization work through the complexity to create value, then you will be rewarded with competitive advantage.

SUMMARY OF THE CHAPTER

- Complex strategies need complex organization arrangements. But unrewarded complexity should be eliminated, and rewarded complexity embraced.

- The primary drivers of strategic complexity are: a) mix of global and local businesses, b) diversity of the product portfolio, and c) extent of strategic growth horizons.

- Rewarded complexity reflects the value that is extracted from a company's assets at the *connection points* across business units, markets, and functions.

- Rewarded complexity often makes doing business easier for customers (e.g., customer-focused business units and key account management), but more challenging for managers who must work together to resolve points of tension.

- Unrewarded complexity is often the product of excess layers, misalignments between structure and process and rewards, as well as overlapping roles, and confused decision rights.

CHAPTER 3

The Five Activators

The operating model is the organizational expression of a company's strategy, but it is just an aspiration until it is brought to life and new work, decisions, and outcomes are achieved. Business leaders and human resource and organization development professionals have become quite sophisticated about the implementation and change management work required to move from one operating model to another. New roles are defined, talent is moved, decision rights are mapped, and business processes and information systems are put into place. This implementation work to move from point A to point B is essential, but it is not sufficient.

We are frequently invited into companies a year or two after they have made a substantial organizational change in response to a strategic redirection. We encounter frustration that the new operating model—which is often quite logical and compelling—isn't resulting in the desired business impact. Our consulting work, and research with many multinationals, argues that the missing ingredient is *activation*.

We define activation of the global operating model as:

The deliberate and adaptive creation of new work, decisions, and business outcomes gained through the repetition and refinement of management processes and interactions over time, enabled by well-designed organizational arrangements and collaborative mindsets.

Activation is the bridge from design to performance. Activation is different from the design and implementation task. These are both somewhat static and time-bound activities. Anyone who has ever worked on organizational change has heard an anxious business leader looking at a design or implementation plan say, "Okay, but when do we go live?" Activation starts with design and is dependent on good implementation, but it goes beyond the go-live date. With activation there is learning and adjustment that can only come through leaders and managers engaging horizontally across organizational boundaries through a series of real business decision-making cycles, and then analyzing and reflecting on outcomes. Finally, activation is achieved when the necessary modifications in structure, process, metrics, or behaviors are made based on this learning.

Business strategies and organization designs are only aspirations until they are brought to life. Winning in the marketplace is achieved through unique organizational capabilities that are hard for competitors to copy. Activation is all about building capabilities. Let's take a simplified example of a fashion clothing company to illustrate the definitions and concepts we've introduced.

Strategy and growth choices: A US-based fashion company wants to both expand its brand into Asia and move from its core women's and shoe collection to adjacent categories (men's, accessories, fitness, etc.).

Global operating model: The shift is from a single business run out of the home region with two categories to multiple regions and multiple categories supported by global functions.

Organization design: The company establishes US, Europe, and Asia regional leadership, new global category teams, and end-to-end global functional management delivered through region-based staff. "Collection integration" is identified as a key process to enable the new organization model. The collection integration process will involve local merchants as well as designers from across the categories in each phase of design to ensure alignment on the core brand message, infusion of local innovations and tastes into global decisions, and sharing of patterns and themes across the categories.

Implementation: Regional and category roles are designed and staffed. The collection integration process is laid out in detail including participants, routines, and decision rights.

Activation: Over the next 24 months, the collection integration process is run three times per year. Following each session, there is an after-action review and all aspects of the process and results are assessed. Modifications are made to participation, timeline, and decision process. Because this management process has been identified as so important to the integration of the categories, markets, and functions, the continued investment is warranted. Adjustments are based on what could have worked better, but also reflect the development of the organization's capabilities and how the strategy continues to evolve as new markets and product lines are added. In this way, the collection integration process becomes a dynamic forum for strategic and operational conversations and decisions to take place at the nodes where unique value can be captured. This is an example of how a well-designed and tended process allows a company to gain the rewards of strategic complexity.

Depending upon the pace of the business and the opportunities for leaders to engage in various decision cycles, full activation of a changed operating model could take a number of years. The idea that an organization may not be fully functioning in a new operating model for years may be unpalatable for many leaders, but remember that activation is an adaptive and dynamic activity. The learning and adjustment that take place as you bring the operating model vision to life allow the organization to respond nimbly to changes brought on by new strategic opportunities or imperatives. Therefore, the underlying operating model can remain quite stable, avoiding the upheaval of frequent restructuring and reorganizations. The process of activation becomes the way to consciously and deliberately adjust to the environment. Activation is all about creating the management infrastructure that allows for speed and flexibility.

Our consulting work and research reveal five activators for accelerating business results in the global operating model. We believe these activators are what differentiate companies that gain sustainable results from their global operating model from those that don't. The activators are sorted against three outcomes as shown in Figure 3.1: the right connections, the right conversations, and the right know-how.

The five activators work in concert to ensure that structure, processes, measures of success, and behaviors are all aligned and reinforcing. All are dependent, however, on a necessary prerequisite: clear growth choices. We discussed in the previous chapter the many ways that strategic choices create organizational complexity. We have made the case that strategic and organizational complexity are not bad; in fact, when complexity is the result of a conscious desire to extract value from the nodes of product, market, and functional expertise and it is understood and managed, it actually becomes a competitive advantage. Too often, however, we encounter organizations that are not just complex, but overwhelmed because hard choices have not been made. Product lines have not been pruned and energy is still devoted to past winners that need to be put out to pasture. Or, in an effort to avoid demotivating any country manager, all markets are treated the same. Or simple measures of current revenue, rather than growth potential, are used to allocate resources. Meanwhile, functions that are all aspiring to be world class churn out programs and processes that consume the vital energy of operating units as they try to digest them all.

The most important part of a strategy is the articulation of what the company *won't* pursue. The most impactful work of an executive team is aligning on a small set of true priorities that focus management time and attention on the highest-value activities. As part of our diagnostic work, we often ask managers and staff to describe a time when their organization was most effective. Surprisingly, it is often during time of crisis—when low-impact work is dropped and all hands are called on deck to deal with an external competitive threat, a performance failure, an acquisition, or a high-intensity, time-bound project. "We focused, we worked together, and everyone was clear what work was important," is a typical response. Before undertaking any of the

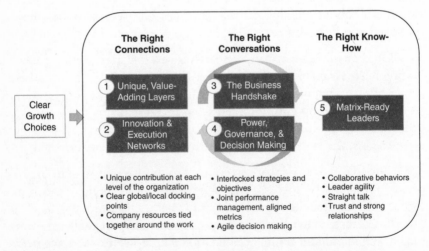

Figure 3.1   The five activators for the global operating model.

ideas in this book, be sure you have created as much clarity of direction as you can!

THE RIGHT CONNECTIONS

Establishing the right organizing logic is fundamental to any effective organization design, but the basic structure options are limited. All global organizations are built around combinations of global products, brands, or customer groups; regional or local geographic market units; and global operating and support functions. These are very important design choices; the more difficult task, however, is to define the working connections among these groups. Integration is fundamental to the global operating model, and most managers are presented with scores of opportunities to connect with colleagues across the organization. The concept of self-organization is appealing but impractical. The value of organizational structure and, dare we say, hierarchy is not about control or telling people what to do; it is about creating focus and ensuring the right information and resources are pushed to the right people to enable good decisions. Management time is scarce, so the right connections should be designed to make collaboration as efficient as it can be (Kesler and Kates 2011). Two of the five activators help to assure the right connections are wired into the organization.

Activator #1: Unique Value-Adding Layers

Be certain layers do not overlap in responsibility to create unnecessary complexity. Establish one anchor, operating-unit layer of organization and a single value-adding layer for consolidating most infrastructure. This ensures that:

- the fewest possible layers are established, which facilitates delegation, empowerment, and faster vertical decision making;

- the primary strategic business unit is clearly established and becomes the focus for clear partnerships between global and regional units, and that this work is not duplicated in other layers of the organization; and

- infrastructure and support activities are consolidated where possible and not replicated at multiple levels, reducing complexity and cost.

Activator #2: Innovation and Execution Networks

Build formal networks of global and local capability with guidance from the center. This ensures that:

- ideas move not just from the center to the operating units, but also across business units and geographies to generate innovation;

- the enterprise can provide strong, coordinated leadership from the center without relying on reporting relationships, for greater agility in the regions;

- investments in people and systems are leveraged for the good of the whole company; and

- execution for initiatives is owned by the network, creating better accountability for results.

THE RIGHT CONVERSATIONS

The work of organization design is to shape conversations. The metaphor of organization as conversation portrays the organization as dynamic patterns of thought and behavior that cannot be separated from the medium of human interaction. This is in contrast to the common metaphor of organization as machine; a set of blueprints that aim for control (Suchman 2011). Trying to perfect the organization as a machine only creates stress, blame, and defensiveness when events inevitably stray from the plan. For example, the response to the uncertainty of global complexity must be mindful participation in real time problem solving, not the rote following of prescribed decision rights.

As we will see, the right conversations require managers who have the right skills, mindsets, and behaviors, but these exchanges can be fostered through design of smart operating mechanisms. There are two critical activators that lead to the right conversations.

The first acts to set interlocked strategies and plans between key players in the matrix, and establishes performance management conversations to drive results, collaboratively, over time. The second establishes decision-making ground rules and forums that enable the partners to carry out their plans and to react quickly to events in the market, adjusting as necessary.

Activator #3: The Business Handshake

At the most elemental level an organization is made up of a series of requests and promises between people (Sull 2007). The most important of these are what we call the *business handshake*.

- The handshake is the agreement across organizational boundaries on what results will be delivered and how.

- Goals are shared completely. The partners co-own the customer and/or the consumer, they coauthor strategy, and they co-own the results.

- An integrated planning process connects strategic plans, with operating targets and budgeting, and, in the handshake, it connects the partners across business lines, geographies, and functions.

Once interlocking targets and resource plans are set, the principals in the handshake own the execution of those plans, from end to end, working across the boundaries:

- Metrics (and reward systems) are aligned to encourage collaboration.

- An effective, performance-management cadence pulls the players together to manage results at the right level of detail, with the right frequency.

- Each of the partners has access to the same data, assuring a single source of truth, and that empowers smart trade-offs.

Activator #4: Power, Governance, and Decision Making

Decision making is the essence of management, and one key to activating the global operating model is to allocate power for purpose.

Once the handshake is set with interlocked plans and a shared business dashboard, operating governance forums and practices enable both agility and scale. This is rarely accomplished with RACI (Responsibility, Accountability, Consult, Inform) charts. Decision making takes place in a culture. In a global operating model, organization culture must support the right balance of global, local, and functional influence, and it must value empowerment of cross-boundary teams. Decision making in companies that have activated their operating models looks something like this:

- Company forums for decision making (executive committees, operating committees, policy councils, and the like) provide clear strategic direction and guidance to operating leaders.

- Simple, co-owned decision rights are focused on the highest-value decisions in the handshake, and they line up closely with accountabilities.

- Partners in the handshake work together with a regular cadence, transparency, and action focus.

- The power to decide and act is delegated to the accountable players, and top execs intervene only on an exception basis.

THE RIGHT KNOW-HOW

The characteristics of the global, boundary-spanning leader have been examined in depth over the past decade or more (Ernst and Chrobot-Mason 2010). In companies that fully activate the global operating model, a pipeline of matrix-ready leadership is the sum of embedded selection and development practices, clearly defined behavioral criteria, and deep commitment to talent development at the top of the house.

Activator #5: Matrix-Ready Leaders

Leaders are selected and developed for learning agility, influence skills, and ability to engage in the tensions among naturally competing priorities. No amount of formal process, aligned objectives, or clear decision rights will bring the global operating model to life without the right leadership behaviors and relationships. In companies that make their operating model work:

- global leaders are able to manage conflicts between global and local business (and functional) objectives across the matrix;

- relationships and social capital—which are still the foundation for effective leadership in all organizations—are strengthened and valued; and

- collaboration and working across all types of boundaries become the cultural norm for leaders.

The power of the five activators model is in the interdependence and mutual reinforcement across the activators. For example, no matter how motivated and skilled a set of managers is, if the organization hasn't provided the forums and processes to connect and have the right conversations, a lot of well-intentioned individual effort will be wasted. Conversely, no amount of engineering of management processes will make up for a management team unwilling or unable to engage in collaborative behavior. The activators also work together at a more subtle level. For example, identification of the anchor layer sets up who needs to come together in the business unit/region handshake. Well-designed target setting and performance review meetings build trust and social capital over time. Functions that are designed explicitly as an integrative mechanism help move talent around the globe, creating a pipeline of ready leaders able to engage in innovation and execution networks. These concepts are all detailed in the following five chapters.

SUMMARY OF THE CHAPTER

- The right organization design is a critical part of the path to strategy execution, but design is not enough. Activation of the global operating model is the bridge to performance.

- Activation is the deliberate and adaptive creation of new work, decisions, and business outcomes gained through the repetition and refinement of management processes and interactions over time, enabled by well-designed organizational arrangements and collaborative mindsets.

- Full activation of a global operating model can take two years or more of sustained management attention.

- Activation is an adaptive process that allows leaders to adjust the design to the current and evolving realities in the market.

- Simply put, activation is enabled by the right connections, the right conversations, and the right know-how.

- These outcomes are delivered through the five activators: a) unique value-adding layers, b) innovation and execution networks, c) the business handshake, d) decision making, and e) matrix-ready leaders.

PART I

THE RIGHT CONNECTIONS

Organizational hierarchy will soon be history, if we are to believe management futurists. "Modern management is nearing its existential moment," we are told (Murray 2010). Indeed, traditional, vertically oriented organizations have many limitations in the new work of bridging global and local strategies, and working across functions and businesses to drive innovation and to connect closely to consumers and customers. Digital consumer communities, multichannel marketing, and crowd sourcing have radically altered both the internal and the external connections that companies must create in their interaction with markets. In their book, *Wikinomics*, Tapscott and Williams predict the rise of "mass collaboration" as an inevitable replacement for hierarchy (Tapscott and Williams 2006).

But hierarchy is not likely to go away in the foreseeable future, and for good reason. Hierarchy is no longer about command and control. Rather, vertical structures help create focus on strategic choices. The new work of managers is less about supervising and more about ensuring that teams have clarity of purpose, the resources to do their work, and the right connections to internal and external partners. The goal of today's organizational structures should be to gain the benefits of both hierarchy, the vertical alignment of accountability and authority, and the benefits of horizontal connections, working across the boundaries.

The bridge from organization design to performance is built largely with management process, aligned metrics and reward systems, and the right leadership behaviors. Activating the global operating model is very much about horizontal organization. But building horizontal connections is more difficult when there are overlaps among the vertical layers of organization.

Slimming down the vertical structure and designating an anchor operating unit level reduces unrewarded complexity and designates where in the hierarchy the key horizontal connections need to be made between the corporate center and the operating units and functions. Establishing the right formal networks enables flow of resources and management time to the work of growing the business. It softens the rigidity of hierarchy by building bridges, and by defining roles and resource needs based on the strategies and operating plans.

The following two chapters describe ways of designing in the right vertical and horizontal connections in order to capture the benefits of both hierarchy and horizontal collaboration.

CHAPTER 4

Unique Value-Adding Layers

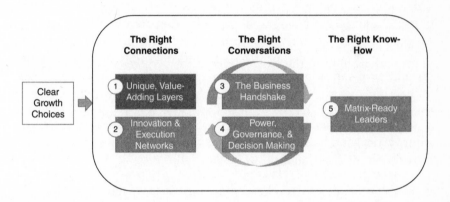

LAYERING AND COMPLEXITY

It is well understood by most businesspeople that excess management layers bring additional cost and slow decision making. As a general rule, flatter organization models are more agile, more empowering, and less likely to filter information. To gain these benefits, executives often bring in one of the large consulting firms to undertake a "spans and layers" analysis[1] and prescribe a specific number of levels, which often comes out around seven. These exercises can surely lead to cost reductions as management layers are reduced. But if managerial work is not

---

[1] Often consultant studies and benchmark data are used as catalysts to make changes that are self-evident. The external perspective mostly helps to challenge historic patterns of layering, with little attention, unfortunately, to understanding the managerial work at each level.

redesigned as part these restructures, we find that cost and complexity quickly creep back in as managers create shadow organizations and workarounds.

We believe that a focus on eliminating unrewarded complexity is a better objective than achieving an arbitrary number of spans or layers. The nature of the organizational levels is more important than the absolute quantity. For example, it is common in multidivisional companies to see divisions or smaller profit and loss (P&L) centers clustered within business groups; it is not unusual for these groups to be nested under a sector layer. Equally as common are geographic commercial organizations that stack regions on top of clusters, on top of country units. These layers of geographic organization are often P&L units as well, sometimes relatively autonomous profit centers. The layering of profit centers is intended to maximize accountability. By breaking the business down into smaller units, managers of these units can compete in their niches with relative autonomy. At the enterprise level, however, the proliferation of layered P&L units is often a prime source of unrewarded complexity, and reducing the overall construct to seven levels will not solve this architectural problem.

A large food and beverage company discovered that layers of geographic profit centers were the root cause of unnecessary costs, poor alignment between strategy and execution, and slow decision making. It seemed obvious that the hundreds of financial planning and analysis staffers who were needed to consolidate numbers across the company were an unsustainable approach to controlling results. But bloated staffing in finance was only one symptom of profit-center layering. Confounded by a lack of integrated data systems and inconsistent process, each layer of P&L management required manual support to gather, analyze, and present the figures in a manner that suited the needs of each general manager and the P&L consolidators above them. The problem became most pronounced when a set of new global category teams, with the mandate to expand local brands across regions, was designed into the structure. The commercial organizational layering in the international markets made it difficult for the category teams to establish clear working partnerships. Marketing people were assigned at the country level, the cluster level, and the region level. Some category leaders found themselves negotiating with regional marketers, while others were working directly with sales leaders at the country level. Others found themselves bargaining at

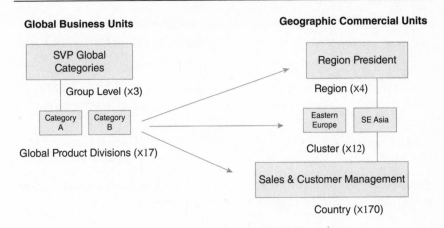

Figure 4.1   Global category teams interact with three layers of commercial P&L units; roles overlap and vary by region.

both levels to gain agreement on a packaging change or a product extension: a slow, cumbersome process at best as shown in Figure 4.1.

The points of intersection among global businesses, regional commercial units, and critical functions are where substantial value is created. In the example above, overlayering resulted in multiple interfaces between center-based teams and regional sales and marketing teams. Roles began to overlap, and partner agreements were complicated by vertical as well as horizontal power issues.

Another example illustrates the consequences of poorly designed layers. Nearly three years into the implementation of its global operating model, a large worldwide brewer discovered overlaps and confusion when its center-based brand teams attempted to partner with both the regional business units and country-level market units at the level below region. Regional leadership in the Americas established well-staffed marketing and supply chain organizations. But the regional headquarters teams found themselves in roles that overlapped with the global teams in Europe as well as the country-based operating companies in the major countries. Regional marketers were too far removed from the local markets to be effective. To make matters worse, each of the four regions effectively created its own organizational architecture, largely based on the personality of the top executive in each. Collaboration across regions was nearly nonexistent. Clean, value-adding intersections are impossible in an environment like this. The result is not only high overhead costs, but confused

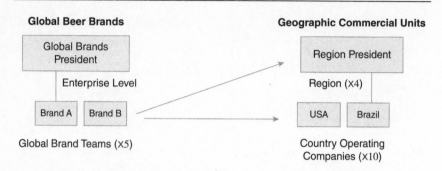

Figure 4.2   Global beer brand teams interact with regional marketing teams and operating company marketing teams (country level).

decision making and disconnects between global strategy and local execution as shown in Figure 4.2.

OVERLAYERED INFRASTRUCTURE

In addition to overlayered business and geographic units, it is also common in global operating models to find multiple levels of functions, both operating functions such as marketing and supply chain, and support functions such as finance and human resources. The food and beverage giant we referenced earlier in this chapter had built functions for marketing, supply chain, insights, R&D, IT, human resources, and finance in each of its four major geographic regions. Over time the company replicated each function at the region, subregion, and cluster or country level. In order to be more "global" and drive integration, a full layer was built at the enterprise level as well. This just served to add more complexity as the work, structure, and relationships were not changed in the regions. The result was four levels of functional staffing and all the infrastructure and processes that go with it as shown in Figure 4.3.

This may seem like an extreme case, but it is not unusual, and many companies do operate with at least three levels of replicated functional infrastructure. Once again, cost is not the only problem with these structures. In many companies, functions are a key part of the global operating model and need to have clear points of interaction with the business units or geographies for decision making and to focus work. An executive in a large consumer health care company described

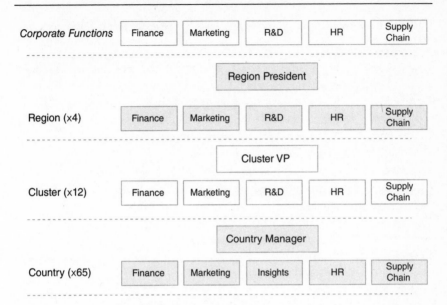

Figure 4.3   Four layers of functional infrastructure replicated in the large food and beverage company.

the problem. "We've given managers way down in the organization their own full support structures of legal, finance, HR, and IT. We then put in dual reporting relationships, and that has added a lot of work into the system. We've got functional employees attending all kinds of team meetings that are not necessary. All of those meetings generate work. It makes for a very cumbersome, costly, and inefficient use of our resource base."

This chapter introduces the concept of "unique value-adding layers" as a way to simplify the vertical organization and ensure that each layer has a distinctive role. Focusing on the unique contribution of each layer also enables simple and clear docking stations—points where the connections are made horizontally for the right conversations across organizational boundaries.

DEFINING A UNIQUE VALUE-ADDING ROLE FOR EACH LAYER

Every layer should have a unique purpose, each should deliver unique results, and all layers should be connected, not gapped or overlapped (Drotter 2011). Clear differentiation of the results, by layer, enables

Table 4.1 The unique role of each layer of organization (Drotter 2011).

Layer One	Define the corporate strategic framework, including vision, mission, and values.
Layer Two	Create a business strategy to deliver short- and long-term profit, based on the business unit's role in the portfolio.
Layer Three	Manage each function to achieve a competitive advantage that supports the strategies.
Layer Four	Use functional capability and annual operating plans to deliver productivity, standards, information, and decision making.
Level Five	Manage clearly defined roles and train and develop people to enable the delivery of results.
Level Six	Produce and execute the designs, products, services, sales, and fulfillment promises against the business plan.

performance through clarity, focus, and efficient use of managerial time. (See Table 4.1.)

Elliott Jaques' body of work on "requisite organization" wisely argued that it is critical to understand the work at each level of organization and to differentiate task complexity from level to level in order to reduce overlap in managerial roles (1989). One measure of task complexity is time span authority; that is, how far out on the horizon each executive at a particular level should be thinking, planning, and working. This is a powerful idea for making certain that managers at each organizational level are not doing the work of the level below. For example, a group executive who oversees multiple general managers should be focusing primarily on issues that have more long-term, strategic consequences than the issues addressed by the direct reports as shown in Table 4.2.

If general managers are driving three-year strategies for sales growth and profit margins for a product division, then the group executive should be managing the overall portfolio of businesses, growing a long-term general management talent pool, and developing new opportunities in the whitespaces between the existing product units with a five- to 10-year horizon. In a functional context the same would be true for the work of a global brand marketer versus a regional and country-level brand marketer, albeit with much shorter respective

Table 4.2 Jaques' requisite organization view of organizational leveling: six strata of work complexity found in all business hierarchies.

Level	Complexity	Authority Time Span
VI	Creates an environment for the entire organization to succeed	10–20 years
V	Applies judgment against constantly shifting events—intuitive and diagnostic challenges	5–10 years
IV	Parallel processes several interacting variables—make trade-offs	2–5 years
III	Understands entire process and has preplanned ways to respond	1–2 years
II	Can reflect on potential problems and diagnose	3–12 months
I	Executes against a prescribed, linear path	90 days

time horizons. A unique, value-adding role for each layer is critical, and it starts with clarifying how each level is positioned to have the greatest impact on short- and long-term business results.

The global brewing company referenced earlier in the chapter provides an illustration. Three geographic operating layers were designated: global, regional, and operating company (country/market). Broad role definitions were provided and smart, talented leaders were put in place. But within 18 months of the rollout it became clear that too many smart, talented people were trying to do too much of the same work, all eager to display their talents. Global brand leaders in the center were keen to expand their brands to new markets, sending out detailed brand activation plans for the field to adopt. Marketers in each of the four large regional organizations aggregated these strategies and acted as gatekeepers between the global teams and the country operating units, while creating their own regional marketing plans. The complexity produced significant frustration for leadership at all three levels of the business, and slowed competitive response to a crawl at a time when the industry was dealing with hundreds of upstart challengers in the craft beer business. Figure 4.4 illustrates the problem and shows a way to redefine roles and resourcing to streamline complexity and empower the operating units.

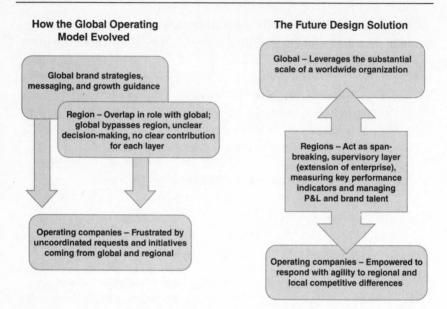

Figure 4.4   Global brewer organization: the problem and the solution to overlapping roles among the organizational layers.

THE ANCHOR LAYER

Activating global collaboration is difficult and expensive to engineer under the best of circumstances. Unnecessary vertical layering of business units and functions and proliferation of profit centers make it even more difficult. Horizontal connections are more easily wired together when units that must work together have a clearly designated partner at a single *anchor layer*.

We define an anchor layer as *the organizational level where the core P&L units are embedded in large, multinational companies.* In a global product or brand business the anchor layer is the strategic business unit (SBU), the layer that is primarily accountable for developing growth strategies and the plans to execute them. SBUs typically own a set of customers, channels, and competitors, with its own cost structure. In a geographic sales and customer-management organization, identifying the anchor layer requires more judgment. Here the anchor layer is the key point of delegation into "the field," the optimal level for making trade-off decisions across global product lines or brands, to grow profitable sales.

In large, complex organizations identification of an anchor layer can help deliver both agility and leverage by effectively reducing unrewarded complexity, cost, and duplication.

A number of principles guide the design of the anchor layer.

1. The fewest possible layers overall enable delegation and faster decision making.

2. Each layer in the organization must have a clear and unique, value-adding role to play in delivering growth.

3. One layer is designated as the anchor layer in the business; this layer is the home of the primary operating units that have been delegated authority to make short- and long-term P&L trade-offs that are best for that business.

4. Docking stations are the clear points of interaction, the nodes in the matrix where global and local will build partnerships for creating value.

5. Consolidation of infrastructure and the avoidance of duplicated functional activity at multiple layers allow for more productive support and partnering to the business units.

Let's go back to the large food and beverage company. The layered P&L structures needed to be simplified. The CEO charged a cross-company team to study the issue and come back with a solution. They recommended that the 12 country clusters be designated as an anchor layer for geographic business units, and management should refocus the work of the other general management layers to either support or oversee that operating layer as the core P&L unit of the business. The region layer above became a span-breaking point for consolidation, and the country-level sales organizations below were to be measured more narrowly on revenue and cost of selling. Local brand marketers could now be consolidated into cluster category teams within the anchor layer and given greater clout and concentration of resources. Clear docking stations could now be established between the global brand teams and each of the 12 clusters. The intent was to enable a consistent, worldwide network of brand-building and innovation resources as shown in Figure 4.5.

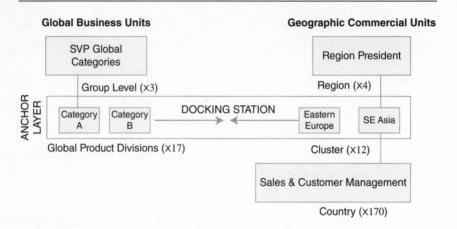

Figure 4.5   In the food and beverage company an anchor layer is established at the geographic cluster layer, with a clear docking station for global categories. P&L sits at the anchor layer.

FINDING THE ANCHOR LAYER

While fewer layers of management are desirable in general, seven or more supervisory levels are often needed to maintain reasonable spans of control in very large, geographically diverse companies. What is more important than the absolute number is that each level plays a unique, value-adding role to the business. When one layer is designated as the anchor operating unit layer and all others serve that layer, waste and duplication are eliminated in the vertical structure and account-ability is enhanced.

Isolating the right anchor layer requires a bit of due diligence. It is important to decide at what level the primary strategic and tactical P&L decisions in the business should get made. A simple test is to ask: At what level can trade-off decisions across categories, markets, and investments in innovation and brand building be optimized for the good of the enterprise, while still keeping decision making close to the customer? The anchor layer should define the optimal level for these types of operating decisions.

When P&L discretion is delegated at too low a level, overall business results may be suboptimized. For example, a local general manager may choose, midyear, to maximize the chance of hitting sales targets by pulling the advertising budget from a new product offering that has yet to gain traction. This move will allow the general manager to concentrate media dollars on an established product or brand that will be more of a sure thing to bring in the needed revenue. While this is a rational local decision, it may very well be suboptimizing the overall company's long-term results. On the other hand, another risk is that trade-off decisions are elevated too high in the organization where accountability for results is diminished or there is not enough granularity or visibility to make the right choices. For example, in the face of declining same-store sales in the United States, McDonald's decided in 2014 to push decision making out into a new set of operating units. The existing operating structure had placed decision making for menu selections in the hands of managers who ran very large regional units that ignored critical differences in taste from one subregion to another. In both these cases, structure and metrics are closely related and past choices had driven undesirable decisions.

MCDONALD'S FEELS THE PRESSURE TO MOVE CLOSER TO CONSUMERS

In October 2014 McDonald's announced a reorganization of its US operations to better respond to differences in local consumer tastes while reducing duplication of support infrastructure. That McDonald's, with its iconic menu, would find that its fast food offering was less relevant to consumer tastes in the various corners of the United States is testament to the need of all companies to be able to meet the needs of microsegments today.

For the past decade McDonald's US had been organized into three divisions—West, East, and Central, each responsible for products within the entire division. As a result, customers in Minnesota were being offered the same menu items, such as sweet tea, as those in Louisiana, which both fall in McDonald's Central division, despite the fact that sweet tea is a distinctly Southern taste.

McDonald's US President Mike Andres said in an e-mail to US franchisees and corporate staff, "The reality is that our

(continued)

(continued)

current US structure is not optimized for the customer. What has worked for McDonald's US for the past decade is not sufficient to propel the business forward in the future." In response, the company has created four new zones—Northeast, South, Central, and West—and 22 regions within them that will give managers much more autonomy to respond to local consumer tastes and preferences. Mr. Andres said in the *Wall Street Journal* that as the country has grown more diverse, "we need to be more sophisticated in how we use local intelligence to address specific consumer needs. In short, we must evolve our culture and organizational structure to put decision making closer to our customers."

Along with providing more decision autonomy to managers closer to the customer (moving the anchor layer closer to consumers), the company also pulled management of human resources and finance staff out of the three old divisions and consolidated management of these support functions at the US market level (a move to a single value-adding layer of infrastructure). "You've told us that there are too many layers, redundancies in planning and communication, competing priorities, barriers to efficient decision making, and too much talking to ourselves instead of to and about our customers," Mr. Andres said to his management staff and franchisees (Jargon 2014).

Business units, as an organizational construct, are fundamentally intended to create accountability for an entire business result. They do this very well when product lines in the business portfolio are very discrete, when they compete using different capabilities, and don't overlap in terms of technologies or customers. Theoretically, each division general manager is given freedom to compete against the best of the pure players in the industry with the advantage of the company's greater assets. The reality of this overused structural device is that general managers are often measured and paid to make value-destroying choices for the greater company. Tyco's industrial valves and flow control business (now part of Pentair) discovered that its separate product divisions and subsidiaries around the world were actually competing with each other in attempting to win business from major customers such as Shell Oil, driving margins lower and ignoring opportunities to bundle solutions across operating units to grow overall revenue. This is not uncommon when country or location-based operations are treated as P&L units. A useful question in identifying the anchor layer is: At what level do we want leaders to have the authority and the accountability for the full results of a business in order to assure the right trade-offs? Getting it right enables clear accountability, higher degrees of delegation (including less vertical overlap in managerial roles), and the right docking points between global and local leadership.

In late 2014 The Coca-Cola Co. announced a companywide initiative to establish an anchor layer and eliminate its regional-group layer to create a direct connection between units at headquarters and the country business units. The changes were designed to "rewire our organization for faster and more effective decision making," CEO Muhtar Kent said in an internal memorandum to employees (Esterl 2014). The Coke system had become a complex web where big ideas, driven from the center, had to be negotiated with each region and often country-level general managers before they could be activated. Unfortunately, it took a downturn in results and stock performance to initiate the changes, largely aimed at cost reductions. It was decided to have the center-based marketers interact directly with countries or small clusters of countries, in order to drive brand building and product expansion ideas across regions.

The Coke example helps to make the point about where to place the anchor layer. Consumer-focused companies must reflect a wide range of diverse shopper needs, especially in industries where there are very few, true global products. The anchor layer in these companies is more likely to be at a lower level in the hierarchy, closer to the consumer. The large regional organizations that sit above these geographic units are more likely to add value by serving as span-breaking units for overseeing the operating units. By removing the regional layer, Coke clarified the anchor layer and the strategic docking stations. Remember we noted that the anchor layer is where authority is located to make short- and long-term trade-offs. Here the center marketers provide the global direction, but in direct interaction with local marketers who are in close contact with consumer trends. In this business, a regional marketing view didn't add value.

In contrast, if you are Philips and marketing high-priced, magnetic resonance imaging machines to large health care providers, strategies and customer relationships can benefit from being managed at a regional level. Product designs for most developed markets around the world will be similar, and variations in design and price points for capital equipment for many developing markets will share common characteristics; it is at a regional level where marketing trade-offs can best be made. The region is the anchor layer, and the country level then is focused on sales execution.

SPAN BREAKERS

Span breakers are often a necessary layer of management in large companies. But the role of the span-breaking layer is limited and should be designed to fit the purpose. A business group or sector layer may be placed over a set of businesses to narrow the span of control for the chief executive. The span-breaker role—often called a group executive—can add value by overseeing business unit strategies, by reviewing the performance of businesses on a regular basis, and by coaching and developing general managers. They do not necessarily need to consolidate business results, and as a rule they do not make portfolio trade-offs across businesses unless those businesses are connected by common sales channels, technology platforms, or key customers. Even when a business group or sector executive is expected to seek synergies across a group of businesses, as they do at Danaher, very little infrastructure is required, perhaps a single financial partner and/or an HR partner. In many cases this support is more effectively provided from the corporate functions. The rule for span-breaking layers is: Keep them lean.

HOW FUNCTIONS CAN CREATE THE RIGHT CONNECTIONS

Global functions can provide both strong enterprise oversight and guidance along with the specialized expertise that allows businesspeople in the market to make better decisions. Once the anchor operating unit layer is identified, it is much easier to design corporate and business-unit functions.

Too many executive teams find themselves debating the benefits of centralized versus decentralized for support functions such as finance, human resources, and public affairs, as well as operating functions such as marketing, supply chain, and R&D. Centralization versus decentralization is a false debate. Today's large companies need the benefits of enterprise agility gained through an end-to-end view of resource allocation from the field back to the center; and they need the agility of empowered business units. Business and market units in a global company are all about differentiation, often competing against nimble, focused firms with deep local knowledge and ties. Think of functions as a counterweight to the natural centrifugal forces that prompt managers to emphasize differences, rather than see similarities with other units. In this way, functions become critical connections across boundaries.

Functions need to be designed to serve as the proactive conduit of talent, information, and decision support across businesses and geographies. This is enabled by harmonized business processes, where possible. When the overall cost of functional activities is managed with complete visibility to all resources worldwide, functional leaders can increase enterprise agility by shifting attention and talent from one business or market to another in order to focus on growth opportunities.

When designed through this lens, functions become capability builders. A key design question in rebuilding functions is to consider what combination of structure, process, rewards, and people will enable important capabilities. The role of a function as capability builder is to funnel knowledge and ideas into the strategic decision making of the company. Consumer insights are a great example. Today many companies have fractured insights functions with resources distributed widely in marketing and brand teams and across regional commercial groups. The opportunity to leverage expertise, to share knowledge, and create a single analytical platform is missing. Recognizing this, a leader might think to consolidate insights into a global organization. But centralization will not necessarily bring better insights into business decision making. If, on the other hand, insights professionals in the business units are linked from the center into a network that employs a common consumer or customer framework (i.e., consumer occasions), supported by common analytical tools and talent development standards, the benefits of both global scale and local presence are achieved. Let's look at this center-led model more closely. As we will see, it is dependent upon a frame of value-adding layers of functional management, each with a clear and unique contribution.

CENTER-LED FUNCTIONS

The anchor layer concept helps to achieve these "both/and" benefits without falling into the centralization versus decentralization debate. All functions can share a similar design logic that allows them to connect into the business/market node in the matrix. The logic starts with a clear understanding of the difference between center-led and centralized management.

In this model (see Figure 4.6), the vertical axis represents degrees of integration or linkage. The top of the axis doesn't imply that work has to be done at a global level; rather, the company is able to use its size to afford very specialized resources and move management time and attention around the world onto the highest-value problems and opportunities. This can only be achieved if there is an enterprise view on talent, budget, resources, and priorities. The horizontal axis is about control—how tightly decisions are controlled with regard to how functional work is done in the operating units.

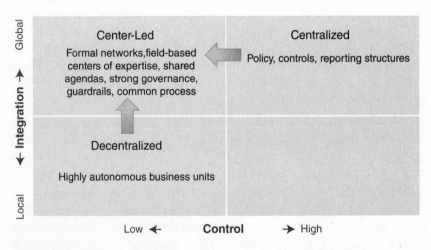

Figure 4.6 Center-led organization designs are intended for greater integration, not necessarily control.

The goal should be to gain high degrees of integration without high degrees of control for work that must deliver both scale and speed. Some work and decisions—risk management, brand standards, big investments—should be centralized at the corporate level. Other work and decisions are so local, such as translations and local promotions, that no value can be added from people sitting outside a given market and are best left fully decentralized. However, in most global companies there are many decisions that require speed and local responsiveness, but which also benefit from being aligned with a common, global agenda. This can be achieved through a sophisticated use of formal networks, centers of expertise, shared agendas, strong governance, guardrails, and common process. Of course, getting the right balance is not easy. As one executive characterized his company to us before undertaking end-to-end functional redesign, "We were mindlessly global and hopelessly local."

FUNCTION WORK AT THE RIGHT LEVEL

The center-led concept is well served by a designated anchor layer. Functional decision support (e.g., human resources and financial partners) should be embedded in the layer where business strategy is set. Shared services, centers of expertise, and other business-neutral work should be aggregated at the highest practical geographic level to gain the benefits of scale and shared resources. Functional oversight and enterprise policy then sit at the global level. The combination of center-led and anchor layer ensures that functional work is not unnecessarily duplicated and that each role provides a unique contribution. Execution can be quite local and often benefits from functional staff colocated with the business, but these local work agendas and processes are set at higher levels.

How is this done? The key task is to define a future view of at what level functional work should be managed and how it should be staffed, from the center through the operating-unit layers as detailed in Table 4.3. A set of effective design criteria is required to do this well, including cost targets and service level requirements. Policy and governance work will be part of the corporate center, as a rule. Centers of expertise that can be shared across businesses may sit in the center or may be managed by business units for the greater good of the corporation. Shared services may sit at the corporate level or may be managed in regional centers. Work that is specific to the needs of a given businesses can and should be embedded in those businesses (Kesler and Kates 2011).

Integrated business services have evolved to become service business units within the corporation, with leaders often reporting directly to the CEO or a chief operating officer (Accenture 2011). Cisco, Dow, Unilever, P&G, and others have built their shared services models along a progression that evolves from discrete shared service functions to multifunction services to global business services. Some of these companies have gained the full benefits of cost reduction and now seek improvements in quality, speed, and scalability to support top-line growth. These expanded service organizations are not just managing the back-end, transactional work but are tying the back, middle, and front together in managing core marketing and commercial processes and elements of the supply chain.

As these organizations become more mature, they evolve from a network of regional shared services groups to a fully integrated global organization with a worldwide hub and regional support units that can provide transaction processing and language support. The global process owners manage the entire end-to-end process, regardless of where the source of the service may be, to ensure roles, metrics, and outcomes meet a common objective. They leverage the global footprint of the company and its strategic partners to build new capabilities that support growth, while remaining close to the internal customers where required. They also gain the agility of sourcing services where they can be delivered most effectively at the lowest cost. The operating units make demands about performance, but not about the sourcing model used to deliver the services.

In every case the objective should be to keep the replication of functional work by layer at an absolute minimum. This means consolidating work efficiently, and it means assuring each level has a unique, value-adding role to play. One insight is of particular interest as we have watched this kind of design work unfold in many of our client companies. From the vantage point of the front-line operating units, the functions that sit at the group level, one layer above the operating units, are viewed by operators as no different from the corporate functions. In fact many general managers will refer to "corporate" as anything that sits above their units in the hierarchy. There is a reason for this. In many cases from this vantage point the work is indistinguishable from layer to layer. Function staff at regional and global centers demand data

Table 4.3   Four-box work sort model for defining where functional work should be placed in the corporate center versus business units.

	Center-Led		Embedded in Operating Unit	
	Policy and Compliance	Center of Expertise	Transactional Shared Services	Business Unit Resources (Business Partners)
Key Activities	• Functional strategy and policy, worldwide • Global standards and stewardship of key capabilities needed to support the strategy • Fiduciary controls, compliance	• Thought leadership • Best practices and measurement • Capability development across enterprise • Consultants to operating units—accelerate delivery of critical practices	• Activities tangential to the core work of the business units • Can be done more efficiently if pooled because of scale • Guide optimal service delivery	• Connect to business strategy for the unit • Analytics and business unit decision-making support • Identification of opportunities for process improvement and insights back to the center • Support/guide local leaders

(continued)

Table 4.3 (*continued*)

	Center-Led			Embedded in Operating Unit
	Policy and Compliance	Center of Expertise	Transactional Shared Services	Business Unit Resources (Business Partners)
Rationale	• Basis of global strategy and approach to growth • Common process	• Expertise that is difficult or expensive to replicate • Execute core programs and processes • Assure focus on most critical capabilities • Help build one culture through best practice	Economies of scale: • Smart investments in productivity • More commonality • Placed in optimal geographic areas	• Allows focus on driving business unit strategies • Act as member of the business but help drive common agenda for function where it makes sense
Value Proposition	Alignment, risk management	Decision support	Cost and service levels	Responsiveness
"Rule"	Mandatory	Most compelling ideas win	Contracted with business plan	Close to the business, but don't invent new tools

from the operating units and generate programs and initiatives to be executed. For the operator, both of these levels are overhead, allocated back to the P&Ls. Hence the common view from the general manager of "I love my (HR business partner, controller, supply chain partner, etc.), but I don't know what the rest of them are doing or where those big budgets are going." This view may be a bit harsh, but it can be a persuasive part of the case for change. It underscores the idea that work performed "above" the anchor operating unit layer should be designed in an integrated fashion as part and parcel of enterprise management. Figure 4.7 is an example of how these ideas play out in an HR function in a very large and geographically diverse company.

At each of the four levels there is a unique set of activities. Once there is agreement on the basic model, the work then is very easily sorted. We can create a staffing model and a talent plan that puts the right talent at the right level. In these organizations often the most exciting jobs are not the most senior jobs, so it also creates a much more dynamic career path for functional staff that may be horizontal rather than vertical. This view also sets out very clearly what teams we need to build and how we need to invest in those teams. The framework also makes very clear the governance processes that we need to put in

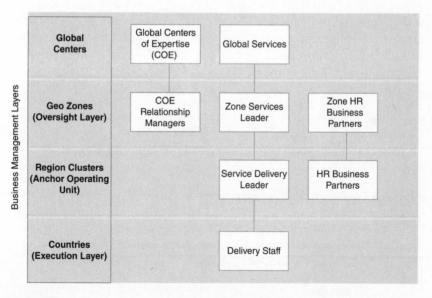

Figure 4.7   Center-led and anchor layer concepts applied to the HR function.

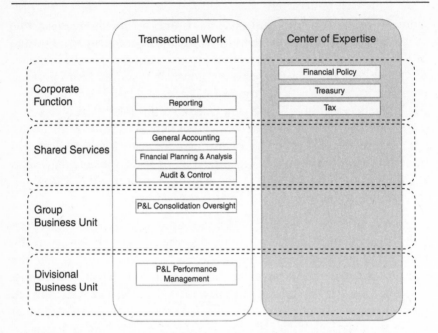

Figure 4.8   Mapping finance work to the right level and business unit versus services unit and corporate center—simplified view.

place in order to make the right kinds of center-led decisions. This model helps us to create not just an effective and efficient function, but one where leaders can make smart choices regarding what work should be done in common and together for the benefits of scale, and where managers should be empowered to make decisions locally to achieve flexibility, speed, and local competitiveness.

Figure 4.8 illustrates, in a simplified way, how the work of finance can be mapped to the right level and differentiated by type. This kind of thoughtful approach minimizes overlaps and redundancies.

SUMMARY OF THE CHAPTER

- Organizational levels add complexity, but it is more important to reduce the many sources of unrewarded complexity than to adhere to an absolute number of organizational levels.

- Unnecessary layers (and proliferation of profit centers) make it difficult to build the bridges across global and regional business units and functions. Roles and decision making become confused. Establishing an anchor layer makes it easier to establish clear docking stations that connect global and local units.

- Overlayered functional infrastructure (finance, HR supply chain, etc.) slows the organization. Each layer of infrastructure should have a unique value-adding role to play, whether service, capability building, talent development, or risk management.

- A single value-adding layer of consolidated infrastructure is often the path to less complexity and cost. Global business services organizations are increasingly common and can deliver low cost and better service.

- The debate between centralized and decentralized organization is unproductive. To achieve agility and leverage, both must be embraced with "center-led" structures, roles, and processes to create an integrated, coordinated way of getting work done.

CHAPTER 5

Innovation and Execution Networks

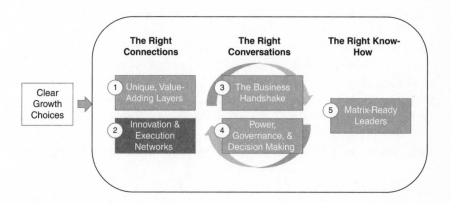

I n the previous chapter we focused on the vertical organization and how to ensure that each layer of the organization provides unique value. In addition, we saw that thoughtful design of the vertical architecture creates a clear structural frame for roles to connect across boundaries and the effective placement of functional support to the business units and markets. The complement to the vertical organization is the horizontal organization—how we design the intersections of customers, brands, products, emerging markets, and critical functional knowledge. *It is at these junctures where the multidimensional, global company builds capabilities and captures the collective value of its assets.*

Warren Bennis, with his delightful ability to articulate complex ideas, argued that the key to competitive advantage is the capacity of leaders to build social architecture that generates intellectual capital (Bennis and Nanus 1997). Many organizational capabilities can only be built through strong horizontal connections. Obvious examples of capability founded on horizontal linkages include:

- *Product innovation and development across functions and regions*

- *Brand building across regions*

- *Key customer management across businesses or regions*

(Galbraith 1994)

A leader has many choices for creating horizontal connections—including communities of practice, teams, integrative roles, and hard-wired matrix reporting relationships (Kesler and Kates 2011). More is not always better. Targeted action is dramatically more effective than promoting connectivity indiscriminately (Cross, Martin, Weiss 2006). Often, well-intentioned efforts to build horizontal connections create unrewarded complexity and have to be simplified. For example, John Chambers, the CEO of Cisco, moved the company away from a hier-archical emphasis toward a focus on horizontal linkages shortly after the tech bust of 2001. By 2009, for any given project, the project team reported to one of 47 boards. The boards averaged 14 members each. Forty-three of these boards each reported to one of 12 councils. Each council also averaged 14 members. The councils reported to an oper-ating committee consisting of Chambers and 15 other top executives. Four of the 47 boards bypassed the councils and reported directly to the operating committee. These arrangements were so complex and time consuming that some top executives spent 30 percent of their work hours serving on more than 10 of the boards, councils, and the operat-ing committee.

Because it competes in fast-changing, high-tech markets, Cisco needs to be able to make competitive moves quickly. While the many boards were intended to facilitate this, their overly complex nature resulted in the opposite. For example, in late 2007, Hewlett-Packard started promoting a warranty service that provided free support and upgrades within the computer network switches market. Because Cisco's response to this initiative had to work its way through multiple committees, the firm did not take action until April 2009. During the delay, Cisco's share of the market dropped as customers embraced HP's warranty. This problem and others created by Cisco's complex orga-nization arrangements were so severe that one columnist wondered aloud "has Cisco's John Chambers lost his mind" (Blodget 2009).

Cisco's stock price remained mostly flat between 2006 and 2012. In the summer of 2011, Chambers reversed course and returned Cisco to a clearer, simpler structure, which allowed more focused collaboration. The firm emerged from this challenging period in 2015 as a leaner, more focused competitor with a return to data networking dominance and substantial growth in services.

Too many lateral connections, committees, and overwrought processes create complexity. In addition, poorly defined connections result in frustration and missed opportunity. Beth Comstock, the chief marketing officer of GE, described how GE approaches marketing: "You have to create a platform that invites innovative ideas. Unfortunately, many companies approach marketing as if the organization does not exist. As a result, marketing often fails because it sits outside, or is layered on top of the most important activities in companies. Marketing needs to be down in the trenches, and marketing leadership needs to foster a culture of innovation that creates new products, new services, and new customers" (Moorman 2013). GE has written this approach into its DNA. Technological innovation, the historical backbone of GE, and commercial innovation with deep consideration of the customer's needs and wants are inextricably entwined. GE has a history of successfully making the connections between research and development (R&D) and marketing that create value in its target markets.

Of course, people interact successfully across organizational boundaries all the time in companies to get their work done. Our focus here is not on day-to-day transactional work or the movement of information in the course of core business process execution. Nor is it focused on those small numbers of mandated global activities for which operating units have no choice or input, such as procurement rules or ethics policies.

Rather, we are focused on how to build distinctive capabilities that will make a large multifaceted organization a stronger competitor. P&G's A.G. Lafley makes the case compellingly. An organization's core capabilities, he argues, are those activities that, when performed at the highest level, bring its strategic choices to life (Lafley and Martin 2013). P&G's stated capabilities are shown in Figure 5.1. Well-designed horizontal connections are often the path to creating these capabilities.

Keith Weed, the chief marketing officer at Unilever, and his colleagues at EffectiveBrands have argued that marketing, as a capability,

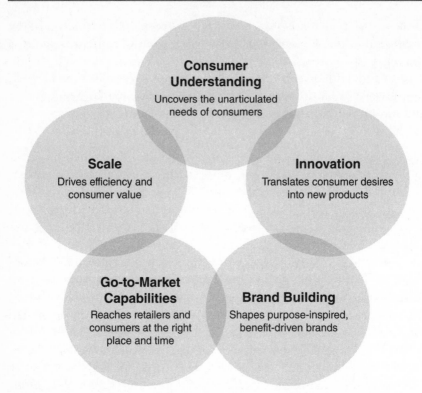

Figure 5.1   P&G's five capabilities are core to the execution of its strategies companywide. All of them are enabled by horizontal organization effectiveness.

has now become too important to be managed by the marketing function (Arons, van den Driest, and Weed 2014). Today's marketing capability can only be fully realized by engaging the entire organization in the brand purpose, by integrating marketing with other functions, and ensuring that global, regional, and local marketing teams work interdependently.

For example, consider innovations that combine the muscle of creative R&D expertise with deep global and local consumer and customer insights, rooted in a clear sense of brand purpose. This work tends to be project-based and benefitting from varied perspectives. It requires true collaboration between those with an enterprise view and those sitting close to the customer or consumer. However, too many times we see managers trying to optimize the handoffs and interfaces between the center and the field through static and rigid processes for this work. A better goal is the creation of a dynamic network among center- and field-based resources. These lateral arrangements become a means of delegating general management authority to teams. It is this empowerment that allows networks and other forms of cross-boundary organization to execute new work without adding complexity. When horizontal teams can convene, set plans, make decisions, and execute objectives, the business has created a lateral organization—a source of enormous competitive advantage in the global operating model.

STRUCTURING THE GLOBAL NETWORK

In Chapter 4, we saw how the center-led concept provides a useful framework for designing support functions so they can serve as integrators across the product/market matrix. The same idea can be extended to the management of initiatives such as innovation, key customer management, or brand building that require collaboration across the enterprise. An objective, for example, may be to leverage innovation investments—to make them "go-forward compatible" and relevant to customers in several parts of the world. Businesses as varied as Nike, Medtronic, and Deere & Co. do this by engaging marketers from several regions to work with each other, often facilitated by a corporate team, against a shared agenda and set of targets. A shared set of goals and common tools and language are the integrator, the centripetal force that allows the work to be center-led, not centralized.

Networks, councils, and teams are not a new idea in business. Too often they are set up with good intentions, but not well-designed, or they are allowed to outlive their purpose. When these horizontal teams are empowered to deliver business results and designed and staffed properly, they can provide both agility and leverage. Designing effective lateral organization is more than bringing people together around a goal. Lateral capability is built through the artful arrangement of roles, decision authority, management processes, reward systems, and leadership know-how.

Figure 5.2 shows three ways to structure interactions among the operating units and between the center and the field. Point-to-point

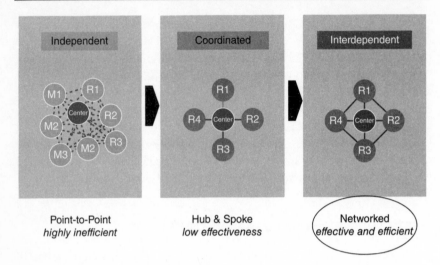

Figure 5.2   Three types of interactive networks.

interactions usually result from personal relationships. As one Brazil-based executive working for a global beer company noted, "I rarely connect formally with the other country managers in the Americas and even less with Asia or Africa. When I do, it is based on my past personal contacts. If there was someone in my role that didn't know those guys, they wouldn't know there are best practices that exist in Africa or Southeast Asia that would work in the Caribbean. I am willing to do the walking, but I need someone to build the bridge for me." As this insightful manager noted, strong personal networks and good working relationships are necessary, but they are not sufficient to make the right connections.

To address this, many organizations create centers of expertise or center-based groups tasked with leading global initiatives and moving information, ideas, and talent across the operating units. This commonly turns into a hub-and-spoke system, illustrated in the middle of Figure 5.2. At its best, the center creates forums and processes for knowledge sharing and pulls together design teams for initiatives. However, these center groups tend to become bottlenecks with all information flowing through corporate with little of the energy or speed harnessed that is inherent in peer-to-peer contact.

The network, shown to the right in Figure 5.2, combines the best of both of these models. It is characterized by center groups that have a very clear charter. These center-based groups need to demonstrate that they can:

- **Listen and connect**—lead internal and external research, find and share knowledge, turn data into actionable insights, and connect operating units together.

- **Build infrastructure**—use the scale of the company to invest in shared systems, databases, and service platforms; remove obstacles so that operating units can focus.

- **Align and empower**—convene and lead the discussions for alignment on strategic direction, brand parameters, time horizons, common systems and processes, and big initiatives.

- **Model collaborative leadership**—provide the tools and forums for codesigning high-impact solutions.

In a true network, the center has an important role, but it is not the dominant role. Leadership is often rotated in robust, global networks. In a network made up of global product managers, joined with regional commercial managers from developed and developing markets, any operating unit in the network might be designated as the lead for creating the content for a given initiative. (Content could be, for example, the development of a new product, a brand-building activity, an infrastructure system or process, or a training program.) An operating unit or function in the network often assumes the lead when it has a major stake in the outcome, has the talent to lead the work, and is willing to invest resources. Some businesses or regions within the network may commit to launch the new product or brand idea early in the process and share in the funding. Others may play other roles, like serving as a test market for the new idea. While some operating units in the network may completely opt out of a given initiative, other units may pick up the content once it is developed and adapt it locally. These relationships are built on trust and a culture of collaboration.

The network concept easily extends beyond the formal company walls to suppliers, partners, and joint ventures. When the Olay team at P&G launched a major innovation program in product, packaging, distribution, and marketing, it needed help to build the brand and advertise and merchandise with mass retailers in new ways. They partnered with product ingredient innovators, designers at IDEO, advertising agencies, and key influencers to create a unique and powerful organizational capability (Lafley and Martin 2013). In this kind of arrangement the network becomes an interlaced set of both internal and external resources with clearly defined roles.

The value of innovation and execution networks is that they start with the work to be done and use a reconfigurable set of roles to assign the right level of attention and involvement. Resources flow to the work. Rather than trying to create static responsibilities and decision rights (e.g., a marketer at the regional level always plays such and such a role), the responsibilities go with the role one is playing on a given initiative. Therefore, as a marketer based in a region, on one global project I could be leading the creation of content, and for another project I could merely be providing input, without any authority over the eventual outcome. Each time, my role may be different, yet clear, because responsibilities and decision rights have been defined ahead. One's contribution is based on expertise, experience, or perspective rather than positional power in the hierarchy.

In this new way of working, no one manager or team owns content. It is developed through participation, through broad ownership, and leveraged through ongoing collaboration. Value is created when managers reach out to others, tapping into other perspectives and expertise. We see many leaders of mature companies looking enviously at young, fast-growing firms that seem to have fluid, self-organizing cultures—Google, Zappos, Facebook, and so on—and wondering how to get the magic these firms seem to have created. In fact, what they are seeing is a fit-to-purpose, high-functioning horizontal organization that evolved because the nature of the work drove that configuration from the beginning. No amount of benchmarking or site visits is going to change a company that was built with a dominant logic focused tightly on vertical products or markets to one that is horizontally engaged in an organic way. However, as traditional companies are challenged to become "digital" regardless of their core product or service, having a high-performing horizontal organization is now an imperative (Kates 2013).

In the rest of the chapter, we share four examples of how established organizations harnessed the power and energy of the network to build stronger horizontal organizations.

EXAMPLE: MARKETING AND BRAND BUILDING

"The single biggest reason companies fail is that they overinvest in what is, as opposed to what might be," argues management theorist Gary Hamel (quoted in Murray 2010).

Consider a large consumer brands company that had ignored leverage for the sake of local agility in its advertising and promotion decisions and its new product development programs. Global brand teams at this company influenced a very small portion of the worldwide spend, leading to costly duplication and continual disappointment on the innovation front. Decisions were skewed toward incremental and short-term investments, which were absolutely rational for the local marketing managers. Figure 5.3 shows how little of the advertising and R&D budgets were spent on global initiatives.

A seemingly simple solution to get bigger, more globally focused advertising and product development decisions would be to shift budget and decision making to a central organization. However, you can guess the predictable result: one-size-fits-none solutions and resentment from the markets for having to pay for projects that have no immediate or obvious payoff for them. Let's look at how using the network concept allows for the total spending and activity to be allocated in a much more transparent, interdependent way.

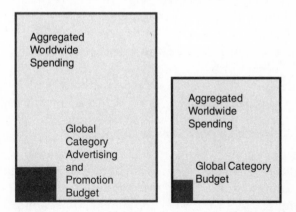

Figure 5.3   Example of global influence on worldwide spending initiatives in a large CPG company.

The organization model for the company's global category team structure is centered on a formal network of cross-functional teams around the world. The goal is to increase the portion of worldwide spending on initiatives that are scalable and transferrable across regions, without necessarily centralizing control over the budgets.

In the networked organization the global category teams act as a player/coach for good ideas that can and should reach across regions. Those good ideas can come from anywhere, but the center gives them visibility through the planning process. Then, backed by robust consumer insights, contracts are set among anchor layer regional partners who want in on a given initiative that is a good fit for their markets. Participating regions work in partnership to fund ideas. Roles of the center and the regions are defined for a given initiative, based largely on where the capability and the capacity reside to do the work. This allows for more specialist expertise to be based in the field but available across the enterprise.

An organization design team at the consumer brands company, made up of marketers, R&D leaders, and other functions from around the world, determined there were four key roles to be played in any product innovation or brand-building initiative. These four roles serve as the basis for assigning responsibilities between the global center and the regional operating units. Most important, they can be configured into purpose-built networks based on the needs of a given initiative. As shown in Figure 5.4, the four roles are:

1. Set the strategy, govern the initiative, and catalyze learning.

2. Create content.

3. Act as the test market.

4. Receive and execute the new content.

Every cross-regional initiative can be enhanced through the application of this framework. The network for each initiative is configured to reflect the nature of the work to be done. The launch of a breakthrough innovation can be handled differently than the refresh of a regional brand, allowing each to move at the right speed.

For example, the worldwide category team will agree to center-led oversight of a big brand or innovation initiative, but the actual

Who Does What in the Network

GLOBAL STRATEGY, GOVERN, AND LEAD

- Center sets global brand strategy and guardrails
- Defines communication and innovation needs and plans by region/market
- Leads packaging architecture
- Identifies the role each region and country will play in the project
- Governs "lift and adapt" of region-led work to the world

CREATE CONTENT

- Leads the development and creation of innovation and communication plans under center governance

ACT AS TEST MARKET

- Tested in local market, based on consumer data, and identified by the center
- Testing in local markets funded by the center

RECEIVE AND EXECUTE CONTENT

- Identified by the center. Regions "receive" globally validated communication and innovation plans

Figure 5.4 Roles are defined for each global initiative in partnership between global and regional players in this CPG company example.

development work will be performed in the region that possesses the capability and the resources that fit that initiative.

Regions sign up with the understanding that a new program of this nature must be scalable and fit for use in other markets. This center-led model harnesses the entrepreneurial energy often found in a highly decentralized culture while substantially reducing the duplication and suboptimal approach to investment that prevailed in the past.

A product development program might look something like Figure 5.5, where the center plays the governing role but content is developed in United States and Mexico and then tested in Turkey and Saudi Arabia for eventual rollout in Asian markets.

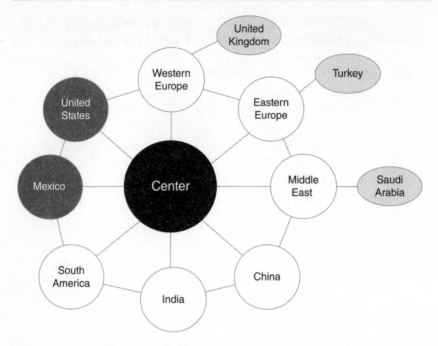

Figure 5.5   Networked roles for a new product development initiative at a large CPG company.

EXAMPLE: R&D CAPABILITY

When Coca-Cola began its transition in 2006 to a more integrated operating model, among its many discoveries was the underleveraged nature of its R&D system. Each of five regional groups managed its own R&D. While the approach produced agility at the local level, it was unable to capture the scale of the beverage giant and led to a new product launch treadmill of small, low-risk initiatives. The Coke culture, characterized by decentralized and autonomous business units, was unlikely to respond well to the obvious solution of centralizing its regional units under the corporate head of R&D. In fact, a number of technology platform initiatives had not done well over the previous decade. Over time, a solution emerged that tied the five centers together under a center-led agenda. A percentage of R&D spending in each region would continue to focus on local-for-local initiatives, but each center would allocate a portion of its investment dollars to a global platform, based on its current depth of expertise. The Tokyo center would become the global center of expertise for ready-to-drink coffees, a mainstay of the beverage business in Japan. Shanghai would assume a similar role for teas, Brussels for spring-sourced waters, and so on. Each was scaled up with targets realigned to serve Coke's greater growth agenda.

In this way, true centers of expertise were created not at the head-quarters but in the regions for the benefit of the enterprise.

EXAMPLE: NON-PROFIT SYSTEM ALIGNMENT

The idea that a given role can be flexible and based on expertise, experience, or perspective, rather than positional power in the hierarchy, is particularly powerful in federated organizations—those where the operating units have high degrees of formal autonomy, yet the enterprise needs to operate in a highly consistent manner. The best examples of these are large nonprofits such as Girl Scouts, Hillel, The Red Cross, or Special Olympics.

In 2014, Girl Scouts launched the "digital cookie." For the first time, scouts could take orders online through web pages they had customized. This may not seem very revolutionary, and in fact Girl Scouts was rather late to the digital game. Why hadn't this been done 10 years before? It wasn't until the Girl Scout system was reoriented from a collection of highly independent councils bound together only by a common brand, to a robust network, that the enabling strategy and technology could be put in place to make digital cookie and other growth initiatives possible.

Girl Scouts is a movement of over 2 million scouts, 800,000 mostly parent volunteers, 7,000 paid regional council staff, and 300 national headquarters staff. During the latter half of the 2000s, Girl Scouts went through a consolidation that reduced the number of councils from over 300 to 112. Scouting was under pressure from competition for girls' time—sports, community service, and online activities—and while still strong among the elementary school set, scouting was no longer able to retain girls once they hit the teen years. At the same time, in 2013 over 30,000 girls were on waitlists due to a shortage of volunteers. The intention of consolidation was to create fewer, higher-capacity councils that would attract more experienced field leaders—people from corporations, health care, and the military—who understood how to mobilize a system to identify and implement new ideas that would make both Girl Scouting and adult volunteering relevant for the current culture. While realignment brought new energy and ideas, it became clear that the highly autonomous councils, which are chartered by the national organization but whose staff are on local payrolls and report to local boards, were still trying to grow in 112 different ways.

To align and leverage the energy and ideas in the system, the role of national staff was completely redefined. Many surveys had shown that the small national staff had neither the credibility to dictate change nor the resources to ever provide enough support when asked. The councils typically ignored national or actively pushed back against various initiatives that didn't fit their goals or needs. Anna Maria Chavez was hired as CEO in 2011 and began a redesign and reconceptualization of national not as the "headquarters" but as the center of a network of expertise tasked with unlocking the power of the movement. National's role was now to connect and convene, identify ideas in the field and pilot them, and replicate and scale. "Codesign" and "moving at the speed of the girl" became essential parts of the new language.

The national staff convened meetings with council CEOs and COOs with a completely new feel. These were working sessions that used the knowledge of the councils and didn't start with the premise that national staff had the answers. Diane Oettinger-Myracle, Girl Scouts' former strategic change and innovation architect, notes, "We identified issues and opportunities together, and then built 'coalitions of the willing' to move from idea to action. These communities harnessed resources and focused attention on the most important priorities to the field. Councils that could not or would not participate during the definition and pilot stages were always welcome to join in the future." The system aligned on a set of priorities, perhaps most important a national strategy for technology to engage girls where they were actually spending their time.

The digital cookie was designed with input not only from council staff, but also girls and volunteers. The idea of online cookie sales was not new, of course, but had always been thwarted by the inability of the movement to align on decisions regarding technology, security, information sharing, what to make mandatory, and what to leave to councils, troops, and even to the girl. In the new organization, the governance and infrastructure barriers were worked through collaboratively to solve these issues. For example, the councils aligned on having a national Girl Scout Cookie Day, which garnered more media publicity in 2015 than any campaign had in the past. The digital cookie initiative had multiple objectives. Foremost was building girls' ecommerce skills. Each girl customizes her own Web page, manages a dashboard with her goals, creates a video explaining the process to customers, and manages her customer contacts. As important, it is a way to keep girls engaged with scouting through the middle school years.

National, with input from councils, determined a common set of technology platforms that the movement would invest in and migrate to. Previously, each council had its own website and kept its own data on girls and volunteers. The technology platform was tested in 2014 and then 2015 became the pilot year for digital cookie. Fifty councils participated on a voluntary basis and formed a community of learning. The feedback will be used to improve the process as other councils come on board.

The network and codesign model has been used for other initiatives, including improving the volunteer experience. The Minnesota River Valley Council had invested in Salesforce.com to reduce the onboarding and ongoing paperwork that was routinely cited in volunteer surveys as a huge dissatisfier in their experience. The technology team at the national level gave resources to the council to prove out the concept, serving as an internal venture capital fund to seed and nurture field-based innovations. They showed that the volunteer recruitment process could be reduced from two months to 70 minutes. Five other councils with similar needs then put themselves forward to be beta testers of what could be a national platform. Using the same construct as the consumer brands company described above, the councils now play roles as content generators, testers, and receivers of various initiatives. Compelling ideas and solutions that solve real problems and are fit to the diversity of council need now drive the movement's agenda. For example, an online volunteer toolkit is available to all councils that migrate to the national Web platform. Rather than try to mandate such a conversion, national is driving integration by providing compelling products and services that are relevant to the field. Conversations that resulted in frustration and conflict in the past are now possible with the reconceptualization of the role of headquarters, the formalization of horizontal connections, and leadership that understands how to harness the energy of a dynamic system. Nhadine Leung, chief governance officer, summarizes the change this way: "We've built healthy systemic relationships that allow us to scale and leverage to truly be one movement." In 2015 Girl Scouts was named by Fast Company as one of the 10 most innovative nonprofits in the world.

EXAMPLE: DIGITAL CAPABILITY

GlaxoSmithKline Consumer Healthcare (GSKCH) is the world's largest manufacturer and marketer of over-the-counter health care products. As part of a larger pharmaceutical company, GSKCH has the opportunity to bring real science into what it calls "fast-moving consumer health care." As of 2012, however, the "fast-moving" part of the vision was largely aspirational. The business had recently organized into four global categories—wellness, oral health, skin health, and nutrition—which served as home to many well-known brands such as Sensodyne, Panadol, and Tums. Five regions served as commercial units. Although everyone was working hard at working together, leaders complained of friction across the category/market interface.

A major source of tension was how to move more quickly into digital—marketing, social media, customer engagement, consumer insights, and e-commerce. Digital is an excellent example of the challenges of creating more horizontal ways of working. It spans marketing and technology and has to have feet firmly in both functions. It benefits from a strong enterprise direction for brand consistency, risk management, and dissemination of fast-evolving tools and best practices. But digital needs to be close to the consumer and delivered in a very local cultural and market context. Decision cycles are measured in hours, not weeks. For traditional companies that have perfected vertical decision making within product lines or geographies, digital is a difficult capability to build.

The Situation

At GSKCH, the friction in the system between category and market regarding digital highlighted the need to accelerate to a more mature management model. A strong culture of collaboration had not yet been built. The category model was still in its infancy, and clear ways of working and compliance to these expectations still needed to be embedded. For example, markets felt that the category often didn't deliver marketing campaign assets on time. Conversely, the category would find that after investing in the development of assets in concert with a set of markets, one market would decide to go their own way, undermining the financial model and diluting the equity of the brand effort.

The GSKCH leadership team determined that a thoughtful focus on improving the working relationship in the digital realm could serve as a model for other areas of decision making such as innovation, product launches, and priority setting across category and market. A survey in 2012 found plenty of digital activity. Many experiments and innovations were happening in the markets but not being surfaced and adopted, as this was not yet an embedded way of working or actively reinforced and rewarded. For example, marketers in the U.K. created a successful forum for mothers called Mum.net. However, outside of ad hoc conversations, there was no mechanism to share the learning from this effort and allow marketers to build on the experience when designing consumer forums in other categories.

The markets and categories weren't completely on their own. A small technical group had been set up at the corporate center in London to spur and guide digital activities. The team developed a digital playbook and other "rules of the road" documents to help clarify compliance requirements, process, and decision rights. Although very well done and actively publicized, most marketers out in the field were unaware of the document or ignored it. It was a typical center product—important to the enterprise, but it did not help the business make money today.

The big opportunity for the center was to serve as a catalyst to create a dynamic network between and across the categories and markets to allow them to solve real problems together. Although tremendous energy had been unleashed for digital through leadership encouragement, there was still too much "hub and spoke." The markets felt constrained by the speed at which the global categories could develop direction and relevant content. At the same time, the categories lacked a mechanism to leverage the talent and energy that was embedded in the market. The function, such as it was at the center, didn't play an impactful role.

Worse, a reliance on external agencies for digital strategy, creative, and, in some instances, delivery, slowed development of internal digital competence. This also created duplication and escalated cost as categories and markets contracted independently for services.

In December 2013, the GSKCH leadership team launched a concerted, multifaceted effort built around the idea of designing digital as a network, with clear attention paid to structure and roles, processes and partnerships, learning, and talent.

Structure

A digital transformation program office was put into place. Very deliberately, the executive team decided against hiring a chief digital officer or creating a new function at corporate that would seek to amass power and control. Rather, a small team of experienced digital leaders was given the express task to promote learning and build capability, with the idea that the program would be dissolved once digital became an embedded way of work and was no longer a conscious effort. As Leo Miller, head of the digital transformation program, characterized the role: "The center was to be the agitator, not the solution. Our mantra is that we do the hard work to make it simple for others. We measure our success by how many compelling ideas and work we spread. We influence, but we don't control so we have to organically go with who is interested." Leaders with this mindset don't see themselves as leading centers of excellence, but rather communities of expertise.

Both the markets and category marketers wanted this center group to serve as the hub for the "GSK way." This included creating a best practice repository for brand-neutral work, aligning category playbooks from the categories so that country-based marketers didn't receive four slightly different directives on social media practices, and serving as the catalyst for scaling proven initiatives. For example, a Facebook page for a brand in Portugal might work well and the brand leader will want to roll it out in Spain and Italy, but the category might not have resources. Or the category would like to develop version 2.0 of a successful app but doesn't have the bandwidth. While execution would continue to reside in the markets, the role of the center would be to help highlight opportunities and broker agreements on where to redirect resources to get this work done.

Finally, there was a lot of energy for the center to accelerate the pace at which the organization could get digital work done. Even when skills and knowledge were present in the category and market, time and capacity were limiting factors. The center was seen as a mechanism to identify available talent and existing efforts that could be adapted, and provide guidance on whether to build internally or use agencies given resource constraints. For example, it was noted that when money is moved from TV to digital, the number of people needed for content development doubles. The center could play a role in matchmaking in an environment constrained by time and skills by being a conduit to best practices and already built assets across the organization.

In addition to a new remit for the center, roles needed to be reconfigured in the field for the global network to be effective. The critical nodes in the matrix were where the brands came to life in a set of priority countries. In many cases, because the categories and markets had hired digital talent without a common framework or set of role definitions, the docking stations were missing. As part of the transformation work, a common set of roles was developed so that communities could be easily configured and the right conversations fostered.

Processes and Partnerships

Marketing processes also had to be redesigned. Many were designed for the analog age—copy approval, compliance, and distribution of information rules—and were way too slow for the pace of digital. The planning process was also a barrier. The transformation office held digital workshops to help the categories create roadmaps and build digital into their growth and market activation plans. By integrating this new work fully into the business cycle, it became the way of work rather than an add-on activity outside of the normal course of business.

In the course of the transformation, GSKCH also changed the agencies it used. The company sought out agencies that had the ability and willingness to build internal capability, not just deliver services. GSKCH also deliberately built strong external partnerships as part of the extended network. The organization was a huge customer of Google, yet contacts were scattered across the globe. By coordinating these efforts and defining a new and mutually beneficial relationship with Google, the company is able to better leverage the tremendous interest in health care that consumers using Google have.

Learning

Coming out of the highly regulated pharmaceutical industry, GSKCH had a fairly risk-averse culture, with long cycle times for decisions and an emphasis on not failing in the marketplace. To become truly a fast-moving consumer health care company, this culture had to change, and digital was identified as a driver of change. Digital wouldn't succeed without a culture of *do, learn, scale*.

Not unlike other successful companies, the prevailing attitude within GSKCH was that "we are so different, we can't learn from others." The transformation team determined that the best way to build change was to find examples from within the company that worked. These "bright spots," as Chip and Doug Heath call them, would have more resonance than external examples and the company was large enough to have already generated many pockets of success (2010). One of the major successes of the transformation team at the center was to capture real existing activity, not just generic case studies, and turn it into sought-after learning. The idea of communities of practice, best practice sharing sessions, and intranet sites is not new. However, while most are launched with a lot of enthusiasm and demand, they often wither because people who have the knowledge are too busy to share or because what they choose to share is not so useful to others in the system.

The team started with an internal portal where people could share experiences and ask for help. Getting content was no problem. By the end of the first year they had 160 case studies. The challenge was to get people to actually learn, to get them to look at the case studies. The team built a monthly communication plan to drive attention to cases and highlight useful insights. They built a monthly video webinar program—a TED-like talk—where three people speak for 10 minutes on their case studies. These generated active Q&A. Content was focused on the highest digital priorities and needs in the market, which were search, mobile, content, and social. External speakers were brought into the webinars to create demand for learning. A monthly competition was held that rewarded teams that successfully scaled an existing project, with prizes and recognition. The result is what they are calling "bounce and amplify." The expectation now is when there is a great piece of content or interaction, the category should proactively bounce it from one market to another. This then amplifies the original investment. This learning approach also changes the role of the category marketers. They may set the vision, but they no longer have to originate all ideas. They become facilitators in the network.

To model exactly the type of consumer engagement the company was trying to drive with its toothpaste, headache, and antacid products, the transformation team launched a *How to Win* innovation competition with a $1 million prize, fashioned after the popular *Shark Tank/Dragon's Den* venture capital television programs. The whole organization participated. Sixty entries were expected; 220 were submitted. Seventeen project teams were selected to be grilled by a panel of senior leaders and representatives from the Google partnership. The winning team had to deliver on their idea in three months to claim the prize.

Massimo Pavone, who leads the effort for enabling the digital transformation through sharing and learning, said: "We don't leave any learning unused. We take all the good entries from the competition and weave them into training. We continually update our learning with actual experience and with current ideas. At the center we have to move at the same pace as the field if we are to stay relevant." In addition, measurement of learning is focused on how well the efforts from the center accelerate adoption of ideas across the system, not just on how satisfied individuals were with their personal development.

People and Leadership

GSKCH had already invested in hiring digital talent. However, as is common when trying to "buy" a new capability solely through people, the organization found that this wasn't sufficient. A few big players were excited to be building something new, but many digital hires were frustrated to find that the infrastructure, colleagues, and processes weren't in place to let them thrive. At this moment in the 2010s, digital marketers want to be in an environment where they can learn, create, and use tools at the technological cutting edge. Turnover was high, and those who stayed were often frustrated by the pace of decision making and the self-imposed regulatory environment more suited to pharmaceuticals than fast-moving consumer health care.

As part of the digital transformation effort, leadership realized that in addition to focusing on bringing new talent onto the marketing teams, they had to take away the fear of technology for the more traditional marketers. They started with themselves. A reverse-mentoring program was set up with senior executives paired with young digital natives to give them a safe place to explore apps and websites and ask "so, exactly how does Twitter work?"

Leadership attention was a key enabler for the development of this new capability. The question of *how well are we building our digital capability* was on the executive team's agenda every month.

■ ■ ■

The development of almost any new capability will benefit from a multifaceted, deliberate, and sustained approach such as that described for developing digital capability. Network-based organization is a powerful idea for all organizations.

SUMMARY OF THE CHAPTER

- In lateral organizations, people in different parts of the business communicate directly with one another, rather through the hierarchy. Networks should be kept as simple as possible.

- Capabilities such as product and service innovation are nearly always the result of close interaction across functions, businesses, and regions or countries. Networks should be organized through smart alignment of work, roles, processes, and decision practices.

- Networks can be designed to leverage centers of expertise, process excellence, and resources across a company, where the business and regional partners work together, playing different roles, from one initiative to another.

- Global, center-based positions should play an important orchestrating role in fostering networks, but they do not dominate the agenda and should not be confused with centralized management.

- Nonprofits such as the Girl Scouts and other volunteer-based organizations can provide valuable examples for business in thinking about creative ways to integrate people and assets.

- Increasingly, networks must be designed to include external business partners.

PART II

THE RIGHT CONVERSATIONS

W e have explored how to wire the right connections with smart design decisions about structure, roles, and networks. The purpose of these connections is to foster the right conversations that are critical to strategy execution. We have chosen to characterize the second column in our activation framework as a set of conversations to emphasize the importance of interaction within the connection points between global businesses, functions, and regional operating units. All organizational structures create boundaries. This allows for clarity and focus. However, in the global operating model the most pressing challenges and opportunities span boundaries, and it is the push and pull of ideas at the boundaries that often generate the highest value.

We recently helped to lead an internal, senior management conference with a large company. As two of three group presidents presented their thinking on a new organization design for their business, one of their colleagues, whom we will call Jack, called out more than once his disdain for matrix organizations. Yet, when it was his turn, Jack described to his audience how the marketers in his new organization would report into both a segment general manager and the group marketing function. Later, we asked the human resources officer if Jack's comments on the matrix seemed a bit incongruous with the model he was advocating. The HR exec told us, "Well no, because in Jack's mind it's not a matrix as long as he believes he is making all the important decisions. A matrix is when Jack has to collaborate with another executive at his level to meet his targets." We both laughed, but it was an instructive conversation.

The next two chapters focus on lateral conversations. In Chapter 6 we outline the business-market handshake, the global-local partnership that co-owns strategy and operating plans for a specific product or brand market by market. The players in the handshake comanage business results over time and work together to meet the needs of the greater company as well as the local business. Chapter 7 provides insight into how decision making should be managed in this handshake relationship and how the operating governance of the greater company can be aligned to support empowered teams.

CHAPTER 6

The Business Handshake

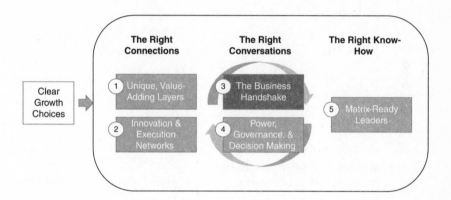

Organizational complexity is rewarded when management attention is paid to the nodes in the matrix that create the most value. Joint planning between a global operating unit and a regional commercial unit (or function) is the forum where the natural tensions between global and local objectives play out to resolution. We call this forum the *business-market handshake*. We like the image of the handshake because it implies that there is formality (design) as well as trust (leadership behavior) in the interaction. It is what happens at the end of a productive, candid conversation where the objectives are clear and commitment is reached.

The handshake is focused not only on front-end planning, but also on the quarterly and annual business-performance management routines throughout the plan period. The planning/performance-management loop is closed with strong disciplines in the back end. The right partners jointly own the plan, its execution, and its results. This chapter discusses how to design the handshake and the processes that support it to ensure that the right conversations take place across critical organizational interfaces.

There are three important prerequisites for a successful business handshake:

1. *Growth plans are granular.* Some companies grow substantially more than their peers over time because of the choices they make at a granular level (Viguerie, Smit, and Baghai 2008). Granular growth strategies focus management attention on market segments, regions, countries, categories, and brands with the greatest potential (Baghai, Coley, and White 1999). How one segments the business opportunity is how one allocates capital (Baghai, Smit, and Viguerie 2009). Research shows the unit of analysis for setting strategy has a large impact on resource allocation, hence the likelihood of success.

2. *Performance visibility engages the right people with the right information.* Not only should business plans be set at the right level of granularity, but performance visibility—the ability to bring the right management attention to results and gaps—must also be granular. It doesn't mean one misses the bigger picture, but insight requires data at a sufficient level of detail to take action.

3. *Business results are owned by empowered, global–local partnerships.* The anchor layer defines the level in the hierarchy for achieving optimal decisions that can deliver local and companywide results, short and long term. The global–local partnerships are the critical nodes for value creation. These nodes, working at the right level of granularity, arguably *are* the business. This is a change in mindset for many senior executive teams eager to jump into operating issues to solve performance gaps.

STRUCTURING THE HANDSHAKE

Structurally, the handshake is enabled by clear connection points, or docking stations. For example, an integrator role within a regional business unit becomes the designated partner to the global brand team, and together they work to execute marketing strategy. Without

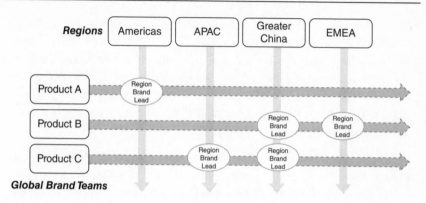

Figure 6.1   Docking stations between global and regional business units.

designated connection points between global and local, navigating the complex matrix is simply too much work, and there is no basis for a firm handshake.

Figure 6.1 illustrates the integrator role. In this case it sits within a regional marketing team and serves as the key point of contact for a global product business unit. These relationships can be relatively informal, as they are in the Campbell's Soup Co.'s global biscuits and snacks category organization. Issues are resolved on an as-needed basis through ad hoc meetings. In other companies, such as P&G and Unilever, they are formalized with dual reporting, matrixed structures. As we observed in the previous chapter on networks, it is more important to establish close working connections between the center and the operating units than it is to establish control and reporting relationships.

While these structures are very important, processes and management routines are the critical enablers in bringing the handshake to life.

INTERLOCKED BUSINESS PLANS—THE FRONT END OF THE HANDSHAKE

The acid test of alignment in the global operating model is how well the strategy is executed. A.G. Lafley argues than an organization should be thought of as a set of "nested strategy cascades" (Lafley and Martin 2013). Strategy gets executed at multiple levels in the organization. Each cascade informs the next, and it is iterative, sometimes doubling back on itself. Integrated business planning in a large, publicly held company should be a logical sequence of interdependent tasks that flow from financial commitments to growth-portfolio strategy, to strategic business blueprints, down to operating plans and budgets.

Eighty-four percent of managers say they can rely on their boss and their direct reports all or most of the time when it comes to aligning objectives. Only 59 percent of managers, however, say they can rely on colleagues in *other* functions and business units all or most of the time to meet commitments (Sull and Spinosa 2007). This lack of trust in colleagues in other businesses and functions leads to dysfunctional behaviors that undermine execution, including duplication, delays, and passing up attractive opportunities to serve customers (Sull, Homkes, and Sull 2015).

Joint planning, the front end of the business-market handshake, requires shared ownership for a set of goals, strategies, and operating plans. The more disconnects there are in the planning cycle separating strategic intent from operating plans and budgets, the more difficult it is to link the objectives of global business unit leaders with those of regional teams and worldwide functions.

Surprisingly, annual operating targets are often set with inadequate connection to strategic growth plans. This senseless miss can cause a complete breakdown in the handshake. For example, sales teams in the field chase short-term, financially driven targets, uncoupled from the long-term growth plan. Because corporate administrative calendars and planning practices evolve over time and become entrenched, activating the global operating model calls for a critical reexamination of these processes. A holistic planning calendar for the corporation is a first step to setting the right sequence to these conversations as shown in Figure 6.2.

The calendar serves to drive greater integration across the matrix in a number of ways. A disconnect between global product or brand plans and regional execution of those plans is common when global strategies are fully baked and then "sold" into the markets. An integrated planning process should engage regional leadership in a review of the overall portfolio of global growth initiatives. This will lead

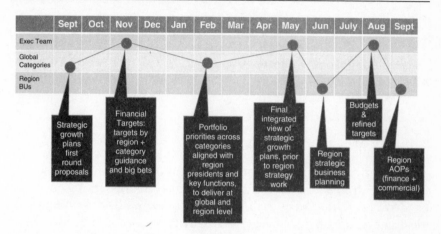

Figure 6.2 An example of an aligned, integrated planning cycle with key planning milestones.

to shared priorities, which will be translated into regional operating plans *and* codeveloped growth programs, managed in the handshake partnerships.

Joint business planning in the handshake leverages the organization's information assets and the multiple perspectives of its business units and functional executives. The behavioral element at work in building interlocked plans should be highlighted. These joint conversations produce better plans, but they also produce alignment and ownership.

When the process works, granular growth plans are crafted through conversations that bring together the critical views at key nodes in the matrix; that is, the global product, brand, or function, and the geographic markets. The natural tensions among these players should not be ignored or placated. The conversation is focused on how we will achieve our growth goals over various periods of time. Points of view will vary, and the conversation must play out in robust debate, creative problem solving, and ultimately end in an integrated plan. The owners are the partners in the handshake. The role of senior management is to challenge, to bring more insight to the conversation, and to move the partners to shared objectives. We have chosen to underscore the importance of conversations because we have seen how the behavioral elements of planning and decision making are as important as the formal tools and mechanisms.

Table 6.1   P&G's framework for exploring strategic options in cross-boundary teams.

1. Frame the Choice	2. Generate Strategic Possibilities	3. Specify Conditions	4. Identify Barriers	5. Design Value Tests	6. Conduct the Tests	7. Choose

The right business-planning conversations start with a discovery process, with all parties asking questions rather than assuming positions of advocacy. Rather than each partner in the handshake bringing forward a developed point of view, the partners work together to discover what is possible. "It turns unproductive conflict into healthy tension focused on finding the best strategic approach" (Lafley and Martin 2013). P&G's framework for exploring options is shown in Table 6.1.

Diverse perspectives in the partnership as well as normal cognitive biases create challenges to collaboration across the handshake. Pattern recognition is reflective of individual experience. Leaders who have lived only in Western cultures tend to distinguish a different set of patterns from those who have lived in Asia, for example. In addition to cultural lenses, action biases, stability biases, and the natural reaction to avoid failure often hobble risk taking in business decisions. Research reveals that these biases are strong and that a behavioral view of strategic decision making argues for processes that de-bias complex strategic choices (Lovallo and Sibony 2010). Dissent is to be expected as conversations take place across the handshake. For it to be healthy, there must be processes that turn diverse perspectives into creativity and new ideas, rather than unhealthy, interpersonal conflict.

Unilever and Philips have both implemented the handshake model. In the Philips Business System, global–local target-setting conversations are structured around a grid that draws attention to the nodes that deliver the most value against the strategy. With its 20 global product businesses (the business-unit anchor layer) and its 17 key market clusters (the market anchor layer), a planning grid can be laid out for what CEO Frans van Houten refers to as the more than 300 possible "business-market combinations (BMC)." The Pareto principle is applied to focus on those 20 percent of the cells in the grid that will deliver something close to 80 percent of the growth target for the company. For example, the oral health market in Brazil,

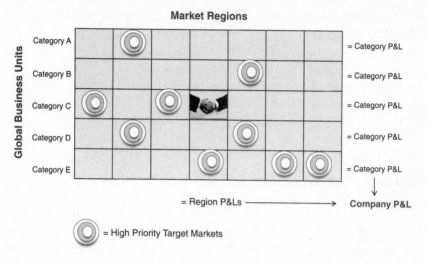

Figure 6.3 The business-market planning grid focuses on the intersections between categories and regions that will deliver the most growth to the overall company.

where people brush their teeth three times a day, is an outstanding business-market combination for Sonicare toothbrushes. To exploit this opportunity requires targeted and collaborative investment in innovation, brand building, and commercial excellence. The worldwide head of Sonicare and the commercial head of Brazil co-own the plan for growth, similar to the illustration in Figure 6.3.

Prioritizing the growth cells in the grid is a critical form of portfolio management that should build naturally from financial analysis and the growth priorities for the company. Corporate strategy in the diversified company includes investment decisions across brands, product categories, technologies, and geographic markets. Early in the turnaround process the Philips executive team prioritized the growing health care segments and specific developing markets in the design of its global operating model. This guidance worked its way to the business unit level in the nodes where a product or service offering meets a geographic market. The growth target sits in the crosshairs of the matrix, and the handshake partners build a long-term growth strategy and a short-term operating plan to go after it. Decisions are delegated extensively to this partnership in the new Philips culture.

We will discuss sources of data in the business dashboard later in this chapter, but it should be stressed here that robust and common data are critical to building joint business plans. Companies such as PepsiCo have learned that in order to do this it is necessary to link up the insights and analytics organizations based out in the markets with a center-led group able to develop deep, proprietary insight into consumer trends and then feed those insights into the planning process.

SHARED AND CONTROLLABLE PROFIT-AND-LOSS TARGETS

P&L targets are fundamental to target setting in a for-profit business, and managers accountable for P&L often enjoy status and power in the organization. In one company, executives like to say "we live by the golden rule—he who has the gold, rules." In the business-market handshake the best practice is often to establish a collaborative P&L with dual accountability on the part of both partners for a set of targets that can only be fully achieved when both partners succeed.

Because suboptimization is a risk when, for example, one partner can achieve in-country sales targets while the broader brand portfolio is not supported, the collaborative P&L is an artful arrangement of metrics. P&L targets will include some that are shared, identical for each of the partners. A top-line revenue target for the product's sales in a specific region or country is an example. Other targets will be unique to one or the other roles in the matrix. These so-called controllables are results that one partner will have more impact on because of the nature of the role. In-region commercial leadership usually has most of the impact on the variable costs in the business, as well as the actual selling price of the offering, which translate to regional profit contribution. Global product leadership has most of the impact on cost of goods sold, which translates to gross margin. In many successful global companies both partners in the handshake have a P&L they are held to, whether it is a contribution line or gross margin. Table 6.2 shows typical elements of the P&L to be assigned, with designated accountability for global business units and regional markets.

There is a balance to be achieved in the way these metrics are set between line of sight (the manager feels directly accountable for the result) and the need for collaboration (the manager cannot fully

Table 6.2   Global and local metrics in the collaborative P&L.

Metrics	Global Business	Regional Market
Sales revenue	x	x
Operating income—market		x
Operating income—business	x	
Cost of goods sold	x	
Selling, general, and administrative (SG&A) expenses cost of selling		x
SG&A expenses for R&D	x	
General and administrative expenses	x	x
Advertising and promotion		x
Earnings before interest and taxes (EBIT)	x	

achieve the target without the partner). The most important thing in finding this artful balance is to avoid directly competing P&L metrics that disrupt handshake agreements. A common example of this would be pressure on commercial regions to reduce sales and administrative expenses, putting at risk sales and marketing plans for a new product launch.

In addition to suboptimized decisions, proliferation of unnecessary P&L centers also produces unrewarded complexity. For example, Deere & Co. discovered after making an operating model change in 2011 that its factories, which reported to its product divisions, began competing with one another within each region. Each plant was able to look "profitable" based on production loads and a tight grip on capital spending. As each division optimized its own plant performance, however, the overall asset base for the company delivered less return for investors, and in some cases critical investments were delayed. Shifting factory measures to cost, service, and quality versus P&L was the first step to reducing internal competition and suboptimization of overall results.

Of course, metrics must extend beyond financials in an effective handshake and encompass market, customer, product, brand equity, and other critical outcomes as typically seen in a balanced scorecard. Some measures and targets may be identical for global and local market leaders. Others will be controllable by one party or the other. Still, they must be complements that add up to the whole.

COMMUNICATING THE STRATEGY

Once strategy and metrics are formulated in the handshake, they need to be communicated to all levels of the organization. There are a number of tools that can be effective in this regard. Procter & Gamble's objectives, goals, strategy, and measures (OGSM) framework may be the best known. OGSM is captured in a one-page document that summarizes the cascaded choices that global category and market development organizations reach together. Danaher, Keurig Green Mountain, Nissan, Bank of America, and other companies utilize the X-matrix (also called the Hoshin Kanri method) for goal deployment. Tools like this are useful for translating strategy to prioritized targets and initiatives, both in the short and long term. The tool is effective for summarizing agreements in the handshake. A vocabulary is formed that can be easily shared both horizontally and vertically throughout the organization. Partners can quickly communicate efficiently about the priorities in the "northern" or "western" cells of the tool. An example is shown in Figure 6.4.

Communication of strategy is also necessary beyond the walls of the organization. For example, a robust strategy for Medtronic's

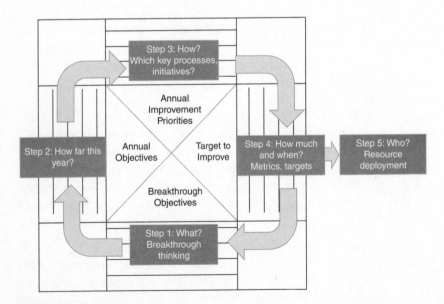

Figure 6.4   X-matrix (Hoshin Kanri) tool for goal and strategy alignment.

endosurgical solutions business only works if customer reps can convey a compelling clinical and economic story to decision makers in large health care delivery networks in a way that fully demonstrates the brand promise. Also, the supply chain must work to ensure the product can be delivered when promised, at the right quality and cost targets. This complex set of events across many functions must come together every time a customer makes a choice. The strategy must find its way into every corner of the global operating model in order for it to be fully executed.

As we will see in the next section, tools such as the X-matrix and OGSM also help create greater performance visibility across the organization.

PERFORMANCE VISIBILITY—THE BACK END OF THE HANDSHAKE

Alan Mulally, recently retired CEO of Ford Motor Co., believes what gets measured gets done. Ford's dramatic turnaround under Mulally, between 2006 and 2014, is a case study in making performance metrics visible to all of the players who must take action in order for results to get better. Performance visibility supercharges conversation in the business-market handshake.

Shortly after Mulally became CEO at Ford in 2006, he began a discipline of frequent and short business reviews with his top 15 leaders. These meetings focused on a performance dashboard that depicted performance metrics on all the critical initiatives in the business (Roberto 2013). The status of every key goal or program was posted in green where results were good, in yellow where there was an issue, and in red where there was a problem. Where the matrix lines intersect, such as between the Americas region and the product development function, those two executives were expected to work together to decide which targets were red, yellow, or green. Team reviews were held only with those who needed to be in follow-up sessions. To ensure a one-team mentality, all of the key operating functions, as well as the business leaders, provided an update on their efforts to solve shared business problems. At the next level down every region and every function used the same review process and metrics.

Performance visibility is the first step to establishing powerful, action-oriented business reviews. A manage-by-exception principle keeps the handshake partners on the hook for results while keeping senior executives informed.

Three challenges to performance visibility are common in complex global companies:

1. *Lack of a common data source for global and regional managers.* When a global product division examines data for its performance in Western Europe, but the Europeans are relying on a different data source to manage their performance, the natural tensions in the matrix become exaggerated. A single source of truth is critical to first understanding where the partners are aligned and where they are not before any kind of corrective action can be taken. Business data sources continue to become more robust, but they also risk becoming more fractured. Galbraith suggests that digital technology, and particularly its manifestation as big data analytics, will become a fifth strategic dimension in the organizational matrix, requiring more management attention and governance in the business (2012). A single source of truth in data analytics is impossible without an integrated approach to data management serving diverse businesses.

Critical data sets for managing a global operating model include: consumer and customer analytics, market performance and development, brand equity, new product performance in the market, and profitability by product, channel, market, and a host of functional performance analytics, from talent acquisition to call center performance and intellectual property management. Increasingly, internal financial data sources are managed in a more integrated fashion through global business services that manage traditional financial planning and analysis resources in a highly consolidated, harmonized, and efficient manner.

2. *Limited granularity and visibility to the right data.* Just as the business plans in the handshake are granular, it is important for reporting to produce deep understanding of performance strengths and gaps, with the agility to see brand or category results by geographic clusters and individual countries. The same units of analysis used in the strategy work require scrutiny in the business review. Aligning the focus of business management around the business-market handshake nearly always requires adjustments in reporting capability. These changes are

not simple to accomplish, and companies often rely on manual data reporting for a transition period until the systems can catch up. Excel spreadsheets can serve this purpose for a period of time with the right data capture.

Data visualization in business dashboards or scorecards has become a common approach to raising performance visibility,[1] with attention to the behavioral benefits of visibility. Extracting insight from the mass of information that is available can be a challenge. Torrents of available data may be more of a distraction than an asset. An effective dashboard focuses management attention across organizational boundaries on key performance indicators. An effective dashboard aggregates data from multiple data points to provide a single reporting interface available to a large number of managers. Today's dashboard software tends to fall into two types: operational and analytical. Operational data points tend to be time sensitive, tactical, and aimed at supporting operational decision making in a line of business or geographic market. Analytical data focus more on trends over time and often with a more external perspective (Few 2006).

A common example of strategic misalignment that can only be revealed through data transparency is the accrual of incremental inno-vation initiatives that stack up in the far corners of large multinationals. Strategic gaps are only revealed through an aggregated view of the spending in far-flung operating units on what may be hundreds of pack-aging innovations, product feature development programs, and other product line extensions.

At ConocoPhillips, leaders developed two versions of their own performance visibility tools, one for the anchor level business partners to manage (a granular view) and a higher-level view for corporate exec-utives to use, each rooted in the same data sources.

3. *Lack of a cadence and process for collaborative review to enable timely and appropriate actions.* Much like the disconnects in legacy planning cycles that we described earlier in this chapter, the business performance management cycle needs to be reconsidered in the global operating model. This is often a matter of simplifying a burdensome series of events that involves too many executives in too many

---

[1]Performance data experts highlight the useful distinction between dashboards and scorecards. The former visualizes performance data in absolute terms (e.g., revenue for a given product). A scorecard, on the other hand, posts progress against specific KPIs over time (e.g., percentage of revenue attained against a target).

meetings, with too few consequences. A different approach to business reviews is required, one that is aimed at:

- real-time analysis of performance, based on business-market handshake plans;

- engaging managers who are accountable and can take fast action in a collaborative fashion; and

- a simplified series of reviews at the appropriate level of management in the appropriate level of detail, on a manage-by-exception basis.

The mindset for an effective business review, in the context of the handshake, should be a continuous testing of the business plans and a validation of shared strategy. Figure 6.5 illustrates a bottom-up view of a performance-review cycle that maintains primary accountability for results at the anchor operating unit level—the first two business reviews in the cycle. The first (at the bottom of the framework) is an in-market review of commercial and customer results, conducted monthly at the market level. The second is a quarterly business-market

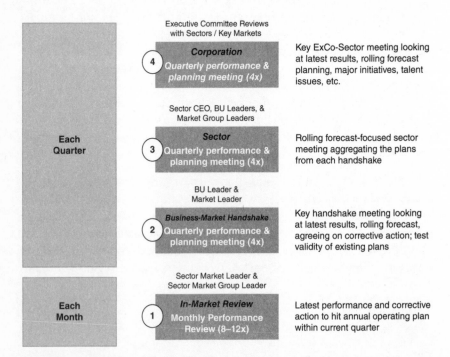

Figure 6.5 Example of a performance management cycle, forum, and cadence from a large diversified company.

handshake review involving the global product-line general manager and the market leader. Scheduling these sessions requires sensitivity to the schedule of the global leader, who may participate virtually or face-to-face, depending on the issues. The third review, which is also quarterly, engages at the sector level in this company, bringing together the global and local market leaders with the sector head. Agenda items in this session are focused on sectorwide opportunities to adjust plans, the portfolio across the business units, and the aggregated rolling forecast. The level four review is focused on major companywide initiatives and adjustments in the overall forecast for the company. Deep dives into specific product-region business results are only on an exception basis.

This business system requires a change not only in management processes and metrics, but in the behavior of leaders. The top executives insist that the partners at the anchor level own the results. Global and local voices are engaged in a social process—a candid, ongoing conversation about operating performance that is purposefully designed to build trust and improve working relationships. Those who are new to the multinational environment learn a great deal of detail about the business, but they also learn how to influence through data-based and compelling ideas.

At Philips, CEO Frans van Houten encourages his sector heads (span breakers above the anchor layer) to avoid interfering with the critical business partnerships at the anchor layer and to practice exception-based management. This doesn't mean that senior executives don't have an interest in these conversations or their outcomes. At another company the top team practices what they call "noses in, fingers out."

Beyond meddling, a common behavior for group-level executives is the tendency to show a bias, indicating that one or the other partner in the handshake is the more accountable. In sales-driven corporate cultures, this bias often tips heavily to the sales or commercial regional manager as the source of truth. For example, when there are revenue gaps, a phone call to the regional general manager is a knee-jerk reaction. These are powerful symbolic actions, and the effect is to degrade senior management's trust in the handshake. A better response is to contact both the global and the regional partners and to ask for a review of product line performance, engaging both sides of the matrix in a genuine dialogue that encourages the tensions to find their way onto the table. In this way, top executives become sponsors for truth and joint problem solving.

HANDSHAKES BETWEEN BUSINESSES AND FUNCTIONS

Global functional leadership is nearly always one of the three primary dimensions in the global operating model. The function-to-business matrix is arguably the most common form of collaboration in a multinational company. Virtually all companies expect that some degree of guidance and support will be provided by the functions to the business units. In many companies, however, this is one of the knottier problems to solve. When functions play an overly powerful role in operating issues, they can frustrate business unit leadership. It is not uncommon for business units to resist functional "interference" from the corporate center, and for the functions to feel as though they "get no respect" from the businesses.[2] When functions are powerful, but not perceived as responsive to the business, typical symptoms are:

- the forcing of functional standards and initiatives in a one-size fits all fashion (often leading to unsustainable selling, general, and administrative (SG&A) costs or low return on capital);

- inconsistent functional resourcing to the businesses (with some businesses overserved and others underserved); and

- shadow functional resources embedded in business units, adding to inconsistent practice, reinvention, and cost.

Conversely, the impact of weak functions in relationship to the business include:

- inability to drive major functional initiatives across geographic and product lines or customer boundaries; and

- inconsistent oversight of important companywide standards, risk management policy, and functional cost structures.

---

[2] The influence that functions have in a business varies widely from company to company. In some cultures particular functions play especially influential roles. There are sales-dominated cultures, financial-dominated cultures, engineering-dominated cultures, and so on. Other cultures are so completely dominated by operating managers that functions play a *de minimis* role in governing the enterprise. A balance is needed in the global operating model.

Deere & Co. has worked to include supply chain, production engineering, and other operating functions into the handshake process between the global product divisions and their regional business units. Functions and regional business units must agree to spending plans, including major capital investments in developing markets. As functions began to play a more active role at Deere in driving process consistency and harmonized standards, the handshake had to be adjusted to make these functional costs transparent and to hold functions accountable for the impact of these costs on P&L and return on assets.

Functions can engage in the handshake process in different ways. An effective approach is often a three-way dialogue among functions and a global and a regional business unit. This is important when growth initiatives require a specific area of functional support from the center. At Deere & Co., in the planning between the global product divisions and the major regional business units for a new product launch, there are a number of centers of expertise that are drawn upon from headquarters in Moline, Illinois. These include the global supply chain and technology teams, which must design a product-specific production system based on enterprise standards and processes. The return on assets and cost structures must fit the business model, so the handshake must engage these functional owners. Early in the deployment of its global operating model, Deere learned the importance of this transparency and accountability. Overly strong functions assertively drove high standards and process consistency in developing markets, where positioning and pricing of Deere's high-quality and costly equipment yielded few buyers.

REWARD SYSTEMS AND COLLABORATION

There is little doubt among compensation experts and general managers alike that incentives, while not the only driver of behavior, do influence an individual's choices. This is true for better or worse. Rewards are intended to align individual actions with organizational goals, but in the global operating model this can be a challenging calculus, and often the greater the complexity in the design of rewards systems, the more unanticipated consequences there are. The Star Model has been widely adopted by executives as well as practitioners largely because of its behavioral point of view on organization design

(Galbraith 1995). Rewards play a substantial role in bringing these behaviors to life, and yet very little has been written on best practices in rewards systems in the context of organizational transformation. Rewards systems are the orphan star point (Schuster and Kesler 2011).

Organization designers seek to differentiate the organization by creating unique, hard-to-replicate capabilities that can produce lasting and sustainable competitive advantage. Conversely, compensation professionals often seek to match industry patterns to ensure that the company's policies are not out of line with competitors or labor market trends. Corporate governance for executive compensation relies heavily on survey and proxy data, as well as peer company comparisons, to ensure that compensation awards are within acceptable ranges of total compensation value. However, reward systems should not only be informed by market and internal equity objectives, but by the capabilities the global operating model seeks to build. This often means challenging the existing rewards philosophy and the practices that guide pay delivery.

Substantial adjustments can be made in the way rewards are administered without wholesale changes in the compensation system. The compensation philosophy questions that should be considered with regard to activating the global operating model are:

- What portion of total compensation, for senior and upper middle management, should be variable (at risk), based on performance?

- What role should short-term versus longer-term performance play in the overall payouts?

- What portion of that pay-at-risk should be based on individual versus business unit (or functional) versus total company performance?

The answers to these questions should be informed, to a degree, by the extent of integration that is needed in the operating model. Consider the simplified examples, in Table 6.3, of how pay and metrics might be applied to achieve integration.

Annual bonus plans in large companies are widely used and can range from 15 percent up to 100 percent or more of base pay,

Table 6.3 How rewards and metrics can help achieve integration.

Typical Integration Needs	Potential Ways to Use Rewards & Metrics
Global product teams and regional commercial customer teams at Deere & Co. must work together to launch a new utility tractor in India.	• Substantial portion of incentive pay for global and regional leaders is based on shared targets (e.g., new product sales in India).
The global procurement leader at Ingersoll Rand is driving a worldwide procurement strategy into factories around the world as part of a major corporate initiative.	• Global procurement incentives are influenced by companywide results in delivery, quality, and costs for the company as a whole. • Division heads' incentives are influenced by successful implementation of the new procurement process in their divisions.
Two division heads at Campbell's Soup must collaborate to launch a product for which one owns the brand and the other owns the supply chain and sales channel.	• Each division head shares the same global revenue and profit targets for the new product. • The brand owner has metrics in his individual targets for brand excellence in the launch, while the other has specific customer service targets.

depending on the grade level and impact the position is expected to have on business results. Longer-term incentives, in the form of fully valued stock grants, cash, and stock options, tend to be available to a small pool of leaders who are likely to have more impact on return to shareholders. These core design elements of executive pay tend to remain stable over time.

But the third pay philosophy question—the portion of variable pay that is driven by individual, business-unit, and corporate performance—is a very practical matter to consider within a given plan year and deserves attention when a major organization change is underway. Fundamental to answering this variable pay administration question is understanding the inherent tension between two opposing forces: a) the need for clear line of sight between a manager's own immediate performance and pay, versus b) the need to reward collaboration with more of the incentive focused on business unit or companywide results. Companies often err on the side of direct line of sight for its motivating effects, but then collaboration becomes more difficult when managers earn their payout by focusing narrowly on personal targets. Annual bonus incentives that focus narrowly can play a destructive role in collaboration. They are likely to have more positive effects when the target unit of measurement is the overall division or product line performance and the target can only be achieved by working across boundaries.

The global and the regional partner in the handshake should each have pay at risk, contingent on attaining the handshake growth objectives. It is not that simple, however. The key question is: What portion of a regional marketing manager's pay will be contingent on the results of the overall region, and what portion depends on the performance of a global brand or product line within that region?

Let us take the example of a company that is attempting to expand a strong regional brand from Australia into two new markets, China and North America, guided from the brand center in Sydney. The challenge is to align the metrics and the pay of the Sydney-based brand manager with the regional presidents in China and North America, as well as the sales and commercial managers under them. We can assume that a handshake has been set, between the North America head of sales and the Sydney-based brand manager, to achieve a specific sales contribution target for the brand in year one. Of course the North American regional sales leader has substantial volume and profit targets for several more established brands in North America. That person's boss, the president of the region, also has a broad portfolio of responsibilities, but will hopefully play a role in helping grow the new brand as well.

A good place to start the discussion is to ask what actions are needed from each of the principals in order to execute the plan. A typical set of actions for the regional sales leader might be:

- ensure that training, marketing, and communications support is in place for the launch;

- fully execute advertising and media spending plans on the new brand; and

- allocate sales resources to the new brand to drive coverage across the channel.

A mix of solutions should be considered in reinforcing these behaviors. Let's look at a potential scenario and keep it simple for illustration purposes. Perhaps one-third of the annual bonus-targeted payout is based on individual achievements. Collaboration might be encouraged by placing some of the three actions listed above in the individual performance plan of the North America sales manager. Another third of the total annual bonus payout might be contingent on the performance of the brand in the new region. This might seem to be a large portion of the bonus, given that this manager must also meet plan targets with other, more established brands, but it may be well-advised given the challenges of expanding brands into a new market. The final third of the bonus payout for our North American sales leader might be contingent on companywide performance.

In this scenario a large portion of pay at risk has a collaborative component. The relative portions of individual versus collaborative incentives might vary depending on the specifics of the growth strategy in a given region, but this kind of analysis should take place. A similar logic will apply to the regional president in North America. The higher up in the organization, the more incentives should be based on companywide performance. (See Table 6.4.)

Table 6.4 Regional sales leader and regional president bonus-mix illustration.

	Upper-Middle Manager: Target Set at 30 Percent of Base	Senior Executive: Target Set at 50 Percent of Base
Individual Performance	10 points of the 30 percent	10 points of the 50 percent
Business Unit or Region Performance	10 points of the 30 percent	10 points of the 50 percent
Companywide Performance	10 points of the 30 percent	30 points of the 50 percent

At the same time, our Sydney-based global brand leader should be paid with similar consideration. A portion of that leader's annual incentive should be contingent on achieving sales revenue in North America and China, at the same targeted level set for the regional leaders. There may also be specific action items in the Sydney leader's individual performance plan that require ensuring the right marketing materials and inventory levels are available in these new markets.

Evaluating Performance. Who evaluates the performance of team members in the matrix is a frequent point of tension and often is a source of unresolved decision authority. When the annual performance of a regional sales manager, who sits on a networked global team, is evaluated, the regional head is likely to complete the performance review. However, input from the global brand leader should have some influence in the final decision. How formal this shared rating process is varies from company to company. In IBM and P&G it is a highly formalized process. Most other companies manage it more informally.

Noncash rewards are important, too. One of the best ways to drive a change in culture toward more collaboration is in career-movement standards and practice. The leaders who get ahead in a global operating model should be those who consistently demonstrate the ability and the willingness to manage across boundaries. At Mars collaboration is fostered through promotions. The first question asked when something new is proposed is, "Have you checked to see if someone else has done this or is working on it?" Conversely, the expectation is that if asked for help, a manager will give time and resources to another unit. There are no explicit metrics or rewards for this behavior; however, only people who exhibit this behavior are promoted. Selection criteria can be explicit in spelling out boundary-spanning leadership qualities, and once the organization sees team players moving up in the business, norms begin to change.

■ ■ ■

SUMMARY OF THE CHAPTER

- Horizontal partnerships are major load-bearing components of the global operating model. Activation should clearly stake out the most critical nodes—the business handshakes—and treat them as the focal points for running the business.

- These global-local partnerships should jointly own their business results, including a collaborative P&L, with substantially delegated authority and accountability to act.

- Interlocked business plans and targets should be developed by the handshake partners and fully deployed across, up, and down the organization.

- An effective business dashboard is visible to both global and local teams, which manage the results in the handshake through a joint business review process and cadence.

- Integrated strategic and annual operating planning and budgeting processes and corporate calendar are critical to activating the handshakes across the company.

- Analytical tools have become indispensable enablers to activating global-local teams. Business teams must rely on common data sources, with complete visibility, in order to collaborate effectively.

- Aligned incentives are an important element in making the business-market handshake effective. The right mix of individual versus team performance indicators should be designed into the pay-at-risk of global and local partners.

CHAPTER 7

Power, Governance, and Decision Making

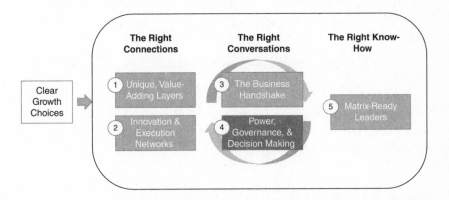

O rganizational power is the ability to influence outcomes, to have an impact on decisions. Leaders have power when they can make something happen. Decision making is the essence of management work. Peter Drucker, who was articulate about the relationship between power and purpose, made the case for a decision-focused approach to organization design (Drucker 1974). But the way power is allocated in big organizations is not always rational. Social psychologist Abraham Zaleznick argued long ago that competition for power is found in all structures and that business organizations, whatever else they may be, are political structures at their core (Zaleznick 1956).

To design the allocation of power into a global operating model does not deny the political nature of business organizations, but it argues we can be thoughtful regarding how to allocate power for purpose. Companies that allow power dynamics to simply evolve, without conscious alignment to purpose, often struggle most with legacy political arrangements. Employees see quite clearly that decisions are made for reasons that don't align with the stated strategy, and this often leads to cynicism and disengagement.

The business-market handshake provides context to align power and purpose. As we have seen, the handshake is a horizontal partnership, a prioritized collaboration focused on a major source of value. This convergence of global and local business choice is the major pressure point in the matrix. Many companies struggle because they have largely ignored power issues among the business units and between businesses and functions. Others go to extremes to define detailed decision rights in hopes of prescribing a decision method for virtually every issue to be faced. Neither extreme is the right path.

In this chapter we explore three related topics that determine whether the right conversations take place and whether a productive mindset is brought to those conversations. After a discussion of how to avoid false trade-offs, we look at how to allocate and rebalance power across the matrix, set up effective governance forums, and think about decision rights in a new way.

FALSE PARADOXES—AVOIDING THE TRAPS

Business leaders face myriad strategic and tactical choices on a continuous basis. Uncertainty and tension among the options are the nature of business. Recent research across 1,000 companies reveals an interesting pattern in how executives manage these tensions. The study compared companies that fail to sustain growth over time versus those that succeed (Dodd and Favaro 2007). The authors of the study identify three pairs of conflicted objectives that are especially problematic as shown in Table 7.1:

1. Profitability versus growth

2. Short term versus long term

3. The whole company versus the parts

In lesser-performing organizations, even when managers do understand the tension between two conflicting objectives, they usually make the mistake of identifying one as more important. Progress

Table 7.1   False paradoxes in decision making are avoided by
companies that deliver sustained growth. (Adapted from Dodd and
Favaro)

Tension Area	The Traps	The Common Bond
Profit versus Revenue	Tying costs to margins versus getting the return later	Customer benefits
Short Term versus Long Term	Annual earnings growth versus invest to grow	Sustainable earnings
Whole versus Parts (Centralized versus Decentralized)	Centralized management versus autonomy to businesses	Overall company performance

on one front comes at the expense of the other. At the individual level,
this is often a gap in strategic thinking or cognitive complexity—the
ability to manage polarities and make appropriate trade-offs.

Among the findings of Dodd and Favaro's research was a gem
quite relevant to our discussion of how to activate a global operating model. Fewer than 45 percent of companies were able to add
value to their divisions and business units through both synergy and
improvements in stand-alone business-unit performance at the same
time. These companies were not wired to gain the benefits of both
differentiation and integration simultaneously. These outcomes are
typical of companies that fail to manage the organization "whole
versus parts" dilemma. Symptoms of this gap include:

- swinging between centralized and decentralized functions and
  practices;

- unresolved debates over accountability, authority, and
  ownership;

- little interaction across business units, as well as between businesses and the corporate center;

- strong separate cultures among business units and functions;
  and

- blame and finger-pointing behaviors when things go wrong,
  especially between the center and the business units.

The key, the authors of this study argue, is to build "capabilities that help the company act as both a single company and many different businesses at the same time." Or, as we have maintained, global business organizations must deliver both agility and leverage.

It is natural that the matrix becomes the focal point for conflict. The tensions may become exaggerated as leaders who manage a global product or brand become proxies for profit margins, while sales and commercial leaders out in the regions often act as proxies for sales growth. Add to the mix a set of strong corporate functions, pressing for common processes and standards and greater productivity. Each reporting line or axis in the matrix structure is a voice for value creation. If the objective of the global operating model was merely to eliminate conflict, that could easily be accomplished by leaving money on the table. The extensive physical assets, people, brands, distribution channels, and intellectual property owned by today's large companies must be leveraged, while individual businesses differentiate themselves with speed and agility.

ALLOCATING AND BALANCING POWER

When we consider how to allocate power, it is useful to think in terms of two broad types of power in the matrix:

1. *vertical power*, how decisions are delegated down into the organization; and

2. *horizontal power*, how peer groups in the matrix (business units, functions, etc.) share decision making.

Delegation of vertical power is critical in the global operating model. The more nodes, or crossover points, in the matrix, the more delegation is required. The objective should be to hold cross-boundary teams accountable for shared results, and this means delegating real authority down into the organization and minimizing unnecessary intrusions from senior executives. Vertical power is usually allocated in a formal manner through published delegation of authority policy, signature controls, and reporting relationships. Many of these policy documents are not well-suited to today's complex matrix structures. When cross-boundary teams must continuously seek approval from "higher-ups" for their proposals, energy is drained from the system. Or, when the participants in meetings are determined by level, rather than role or expertise, the wrong conversation takes place.

Horizontal power allocation is the focus of most noise around unclear roles and decision rights. Horizontal power issues play out across all three of the key tension areas (profit versus growth, short versus long term, and whole versus parts) and in three organizational environments:

1. global business units with local regions and countries;

2. product business units with customer business units; and

3. business units with center-based functions (operating and staff functions).

It is the responsibility of the CEO and the executive team to set the basic pattern or philosophy that guides horizontal decision making. Our experience and research indicates that many top executive teams provide only very general guidance in this regard and seem to prefer to allow the pattern to evolve organically. This reluctance to "engineer" patterns of power is often rooted in a very rational fear of getting the mix wrong, and many rely on "letting the players work it out," or gravitating toward the comfort of a system they have seen work in the past.

How can CEOs and executive teams make deliberate and thoughtful adjustments in power and decision-making authority? There are a number of ways to adjust power relationships among global and regional businesses and functions. Here are five that are among the most effective:

1. One role is elevated in the hierarchy and provided a coveted seat at the executive table to ensure that voices representing future sources of growth are heard (e.g., Medtronic's Omar Ishrak elevated the leaders of growth countries and regions to his executive committee).

2. Budget control is granted to a given position or unit (ConocoPhillips' Ryan Lance pulled all major exploration project dollars from the project management function, giving them to the operating units).

3. A given position is granted a more prominent role in setting strategy and targets or is expected to have accountability for profit and loss (P&L); for example, PepsiCo's Indra Nooyi strengthened global category teams by giving them P&Ls, "president" titles, and a stronger voice to embed category growth plans in the strategic plans of the company.

4. Decision rights are tipped one way or the other for key operating issues (Microsoft's Steve Ballmer and Satya Nadella shifted new product development authority away from product divisions to commercial and engineering functions to achieve more of a one-company view of the market).

5. A high-potential leader is placed in a given role, elevating the status of the position in the organization (Nike executives moved high-potential executives from product engines to running global consumer category teams to increase the influence they would play in the new structure).

The next section looks more deeply at how to balance power in the product/geography matrix and the business unit/function matrix.

POWER ALLOCATION IN THE PRODUCT/GEOGRAPHY MATRIX

For the past 20 years there has been a trend to reduce or eliminate the country manager role in geographic markets. The country managing director role in companies as diverse as Bayer, Tyco, Ingersoll Rand, Covidien, Kraft, and Royal Philips has devolved over time to primarily legal-entity responsibility, a mostly administrative role with little or no accountability for business results. Typically, geographic leadership roles now focus on sales responsibility, serving as the execution arm for global product or brand business units.

The theory of the case was simple: Global strategies required stronger center-based leadership roles to drive more consistency in the value proposition and brand messaging and to leverage investments in innovation and marketing. The underlying assumption was that as the Internet drove more common global culture, then global products, services, and brands would dominate local options. As the world became smaller and flatter, global product standards would trump local market differences. In many industries this was true, and fragmented companies dialed up global product power and dialed down local country management authority in order to capture these benefits.

One of the most difficult change-leadership challenges, however, is building influential global business teams into a geographic power base. Whether global business teams are aligned by brands, categories, customers, or services, there are many obstacles to giving these roles enough authority relative to established geographic business units. Geographic business-unit leaders resist interference in their markets. Functional leaders resist granting budget authority for work such as research and development (R&D) and marketing. Human resources managers cling to outmoded job evaluation methods that place lower grade levels on global leader roles if they don't oversee large teams. Hence candidates at too low a level often end up in these roles, making it nearly impossible for them to establish strong voices in the established leadership culture.

That said, as with most strategy and management trends, the pendulum often swings too far. Those companies that established strong global groups and stripped local managers of power have found that the world is filled with new business challenges that can't be managed from the center:

- State-owned enterprises act as customers, suppliers, and partners; relationships need to be built and proactively managed.

- Increasing protectionism and resistance to lowering tariffs trade barriers require strong local presence.

- Market development is difficult and requires an all-out enterprise approach, with strong leadership close to the ground.

- The strongest competitors are not always other global multinationals but increasingly sophisticated regional and local players that know the local market well and are not saddled with concerns like sustainability and fair labor standards and corporate overhead on another continent.

- Customer and consumer voices remain diverse across the globe, and those in developed markets are more empowered.

The challenges of managing diverse geographic markets are not limited to the developing world. For many American companies,

European operations have become a tangle of costs and complexity as separate business units optimize their strategies with little coordination or sharing of services and infrastructure at the geographic level.

In some cases, shifting power to the global business unit effectively encouraged key talent to migrate to global business unit roles. As a result, the skills and talent of country and region-based leadership were allowed to atrophy. Companies such as Philips, General Electric, Medtronic, Kraft, and others are rebuilding geographic organizational and management depth. But the fix is not a return to the old model, where the country manager reigns supreme within his kingdom. Instead, hybrid models are being built to provide a balance between global and local interests. Product development, marketing, and P&L management are increasingly managed one way in developed markets and another in developing markets.

Royal Philips made just this shift to capture the value across the diversity of its markets. Philips is a $20 billion diversified consumer electronics, health care, and lighting products company and is an example of effective rebalance of power. Once one of the most innovative firms in its segments, the company lost its way over decades, failing to capitalize on its own discoveries of technologies such as the compact disc. As part of a transformation process at Philips that began in 2012, the new CEO determined through extensive listening across the organization that too much power had migrated to center-based, global business units. A decade of centralizing product and brand management in Amsterdam had reduced the field-based commercial organizations to order takers, while the global business units had become isolated from the evolving needs of customers and consumers. Growth had stalled, particularly in emerging markets, and agility was highly compromised, but lack of common processes meant the business was also underleveraged. Philips had all the downside of size and complexity without any of the upside of leveraged scale through a center-led agenda and a common marketing story.

CEO Frans van Houten began to shift decision-making authority to the regional business units by installing heavyweight market leaders in key growth regions to bring management attention to strategic market development and commercial capability, and to build stronger relationships with local government groups and distribution partners. The impact of more empowered commercial teams began to bear fruit by 2014.

There is no right power balance in the matrix between global product and local geography. It is different depending upon industry and corporate strategy. It will shift over time as competitors and customers change. Most companies are continually rebalancing, trying not to tip power too much to one axis or the other. The bottom line is that this is not a debate between centralized versus decentralized organization. Today, large companies need the benefits of both strong center-led agendas and empowered local teams.

THE GEOGRAPHIC MARKET LEADER ROLE

One of the keys to getting the right balance in the product/geography matrix is to design and staff market leader roles with a clear view of the behaviors you want to drive. Today's geographic market leader roles are being created or realigned in principally two forms: One is a robust leadership role that manages the commercial and customer management responsibilities in a major country or cluster of countries. Companies such as Mondelez, Medtronic, and Nike are building stronger tactical marketing teams in these units and staffing the top jobs in the geographies with strong, high-potential players. The visions for these teams are shown in Table 7.2. These roles are full partners and equals to the global category or product leaders that work in the center. Together they manage revenue and each has a P&L for the controllable elements of their respective responsibilities. The local sales and marketing leads are expected to develop sophisticated market-development strategies. At Nike they are focused on elevating the capabilities of the retail partners to deliver on the ambitious vision of new consumer-focused apparel and footwear collections.

The second approach that some companies such as GE, Philips, and others with diverse product portfolios have recently taken is to establish a strong, single-company presence in a large growth market. This enterprise role works across all lines of business in the company to find opportunities to leverage scale, build capabilities, and form influential relationships that take advantage of a company's size and collective resources. For example, a market leader for Russia at Philips was tasked with looking for opportunities across the imaging, appliance, and lighting sectors.

GE's CEO, Jeff Immelt, created new senior-level market leader roles, known as global growth and operations executives, that work

Table 7.2   How companies are redefining the roles of local market leaders.

Nike	Marketplace transformation is the key priority for regional and cluster leaders. They are to remake the retail channel in the top 10 markets to execute the consumer category vision.
S.C. Johnson	Developed versus developing geographic market platforms allow differences in product creation for local market product customization.
Mondelez	After the spin from Kraft foods, executives referred to regional "freedom in a framework" as rocket fuel to global categories.
General Electric	Emphasis on driving deep local relationships, leadership development, and operating excellence through powerful new country oversight roles that work across businesses.
Toyota	After decades of highly centralized business management, now there is a full business management organization for North America.

Table 7.3   GE's global growth and operations executive role.

Growth and Operations Executive

- Builds key customer capability
- Expands funding and capital market access
- Establishes regional partnerships
- Increases mergers and acquisitions activity
- Invests in local products
- Leads market innovation and development
- Invests in manufacturing and services

across all of GE's product divisions in each large growth market. (See Table 7.3.) "With more integrated local teams," Immelt argued, "we will be a better and more competitive global company with more local business development, customer support, research and product development" ("GE Names Vice Chairman John Rice to Lead GE Global Growth & Operations" 2010).

The role of these executives is summarized in Table 7.3.

Enterprise market leader roles do not manage the P&Ls of the business units at GE or Philips. Those remain the domain of global business units, partnered up with strong local commercial and customer teams. The emphasis of the enterprise market leader role is carefully prescribed to avoid unnecessary tension. Make no mistake, however, results are expected in:

- cross-sector growth strategy development (e.g., shared technology);

- nurturing invisible assets such as customer relationships, partner development, and government relations;

- ways to make physical assets more productive (e.g., shared footprints and infrastructure); and

- leveraging market knowledge and capabilities.

POWER ALLOCATION IN THE BUSINESS/FUNCTION MATRIX

Role clarity and confused decision rights can be just as difficult in the business-to-function matrix relationship as it is among peer business units. Deere & Co. set high expectations for the role of global functions in the rollout of its three-dimensional global operating model. Marketing, production engineering, quality, and other operating functions were designed and staffed to be heavy players in collaboration with global products groups and regional markets. Reporting relationships were hard-lined back to the center for these groups, and substantial resource control was granted in order to drive process consistency.

Of course, as with any structure, there are trade-offs. The risk with lack of overly strong functions is lack of responsiveness from the center. As power is shifted to the center with the mandate to integrate and create consistency where variation doesn't add value, the center tends to dictate. Rather than enabling the business units, the center becomes a bottleneck, slowing decision making and constraining ideas and innovation. The cause of this predictable and negative consequence of shifting power is a lack of clarity regarding the role of the center. Merely defining a center/field split is too simplistic. In fact, the term *center* does not have to refer to work and people who sit in the corporate offices at all. Companies are becoming more creative about leaving centers of know-how out in the geographies, where they remain close to the businesses, customers, and employees. Centers of excellence, meaning corporate groups setting policy and designing programs, are evolving to communities of expertise, with members colocated with the business and close to the customer. This helps to reframe the centralized versus decentralized controversy into a more useful discussion. When the role of the center is articulated clearly and then staffed appropriately, the center becomes an enabler of strategy rather than the to-be-tolerated overhead it is too often regarded as.

GOVERNANCE FORUMS

In order for leaders to succeed in a global operating model, the boundaries for decision making should be clear. Let's reconsider the four kinds of operating governance models we examined in Chapter 2. These four represent a continuum, ranging from high to low degrees of integration as shown in Table 7.4.

The complexity of the business portfolio has some influence on which model makes the most sense, but companies with similar profiles often choose very different operating models. P&G operates the second model, with a highly integrated approach to managing its diverse businesses, guided by strong, center-led, global brand teams. In contrast, Unilever is more of a hybrid, with less center-based guidance and more local market-based governance.

The choice of operating governance informs the kind of decision forums that are needed. In the more integrated model, companywide policy, portfolio, and strategy groups are important. The launch of a global operating model warrants a thoughtful examination of existing decision-making forums and clarity about the role each plays, and the way they interact to create an environment for empowered teams to work together across boundaries. Common governance forums include:

- executive committees (the top leadership of the company, usually direct reports to the CEO);

Table 7.4 Four types of operating governance and degrees of integration.

	Fully Integrated (Single Business)	Divisional (Closely Related)	Hybrid (Loosely Related)	Holding Company (Conglomerate)
Strategy	Single strategy guides all P&L units with minor variations	Complementary business portfolio and core strategies with synergies	Diverse, relatively autonomous businesses with limited synergies	Structuring cheap finance, buying and selling separate assets
Governance & Organizational Design	Direction comes from organizational center All process and practices are common Single culture	Control of certain key functions to drive scale, common process and policy consistency Often matrixed front and back ops	Facilitating some scale benefits and some best practices across otherwise stand-alone businesses' capital, talent, and knowledge	Appointing the best people to run the businesses Business units return financials to parent No common processes Multiple cultures
Leadership Talent	Single talent pool for leadership jobs Numerous synergies expected	High degrees of cross-organization movement of talent with common process and metrics	Limited planned movement of talent across units at senior levels	No movement of talent across units No synergies expected
Rewards Philosophy	Single design, limited need for variations Central administration	Single design, with variations in practices as necessary Mixed administration	Harmonized variations in design with business unit administration	High variability; no need for harmonization
Company Examples	Apple, Cisco, Coca-Cola, Toyota, Marriott	P&G, IBM, Danone, PepsiCo	GE, Philips, Unilever, Johnson & Johnson	Berkshire Hathaway, Private Equity

- operating committees (often an extension of the executive committee that acts as a broader set of eyes and ears into the market that may bring recommendations to the executive team);

- strategic portfolio planning committees (e.g., a group that makes recommendations or decisions on new product development and innovation investments, against the enterprise strategy and capacity constraints; similar groups may govern IT investments across the company); and

- councils (e.g., cross-business groups that set functional policy for work such as marketing, customer experience, capability building, or talent management).

The roles that these generic groups play are not the same from company to company, so each needs to be defined clearly for a given context. The decision-making role of the top team is distinct from the ongoing management of the separate businesses. The governing role of executive groups should focus on nonroutine and ambiguous problems and trade-offs, often among hard-to-compare demands and opportunities. When leaders come to the table in their enterprise governance role, they are no longer advocates for their unit, but arbitrating, as a group, among competing objectives. The governance task for executive teams includes the following:

- determining and monitoring corporate identity and mission— why does the company exist, who does it serve, what is our corporate strategy?

- effectively managing trade-offs between constituencies—how do we balance the objectives of customer, shareholder, employee, compliance, and stakeholders?

- setting policy, practices, and decision rules—what are the boundaries that all units operate within?

- resolving conflicts between units—what are our expectations of consistency, shared resources, and interdependencies?

- ensuring current and future executive capability—are the right people being developed to run the company in the future?

WHAT EXECUTIVE TEAMS REALLY DO

Research conducted during the past decade shows that the roles—and even the roster—of senior management teams can be far from self-evident, even to those who serve on them (Frisch 2011). The research revealed that executive committees of direct reports to the CEO rarely act as the key decision-making forum in most companies. There are many reasons for this, including the tendency of CEOs to rely more on an inner group or kitchen cabinet as close counsel, and the inherent challenges of large teams to make aligned decisions. The author argues that instead there are three key roles that executive committees of large corporations can and should play:

1. establish a common worldview as the basis for decision making.

2. broadly prioritize initiatives.

3. allocate resources and manage dependencies.

Having key business units and functions represented creates a good forum for discussions on the relative importance of potential courses of action and opportunity costs among them. These discussions can prevent serious misalignment.

A major petroleum company surveyed a cross section of 35 general managers and senior functional leaders with the aim of prioritizing companywide initiatives. The survey revealed very little alignment among the players in terms of which corporate initiatives deserved time and attention. Past efforts to rank order initiatives had not been any more effective; the explanation provided by most in follow-up interviewees was twofold: 1) many initiatives were kept off the ranking list by their owners who preferred to avoid the scrutiny, and 2) the executive committee was reluctant to make choices among those that were on the list. This lack of candor and reluctance to make choices at the top levels causes decision making to be more difficult for operating managers out in the businesses.

At Covidien (now part of Medtronic), CEO Joe Almeida created two groups—the operating committee and the executive committee—to optimize inclusion and decisiveness. Each was assigned a different membership and role with clear remit. The operating committee debated and narrowed proposals with cross-unit implications that came from the business units and functions. This analysis fed into the executive committee decision process. The operating committee also took decisions coming out of the executive committee and collectively ensured alignment and coordination for implementation.

This flow of executive work at Covidien is illustrated below in Figure 7.1.

Table 7.5 summarizes a number of forums utilized today in a handful of companies.

DECISION RIGHTS

The business-market handshake should be the focus of decision clarity. It is the node in the matrix where a handful of high-value decisions must be made jointly and in a manner that avoids the traps of short versus long term, revenue versus profit, and global versus local.

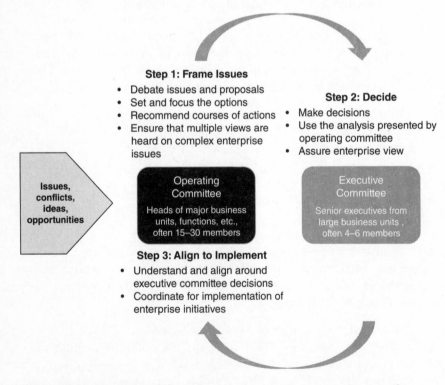

Step 1: Frame Issues
- Debate issues and proposals
- Set and focus the options
- Recommend courses of actions
- Ensure that multiple views are heard on complex enterprise issues

Step 2: Decide
- Make decisions
- Use the analysis presented by operating committee
- Assure enterprise view

Issues, conflicts, ideas, opportunities

Operating Committee
Heads of major business units, functions, etc., often 15–30 members

Executive Committee
Senior executives from large business units, often 4–6 members

Step 3: Align to Implement
- Understand and align around executive committee decisions
- Coordinate for implementation of enterprise initiatives

Figure 7.1   Example of the roles of an operating committee and executive committee (at Covidien).

Table 7.5 Examples of governance forums in four global companies.

Company	Forum	Function
Intel—"Subgroups"	Management committee meeting (MCM) includes multiple levels of management based on role content versus direct reporting relationships. It is a large group, and members of the MCM formally report to other, more senior members of MCM.	The MCM meets to discuss and debate issues monthly and focuses on reviewing recommendations and setting broad direction. It has longer extended meetings on a quarterly basis. Smaller subgroups of the MCM are chartered to lead specific strategies within the company and are empowered to make decisions on those issues.
McKesson— "Shared Service Governance Layer"	Includes all operating team members and business unit (BU) presidents. The chair is a BU president, and this role rotates.	Charter is to approve all initiatives that have a financial impact on the operating units (specifically, an allocation impact). This body affords every business the opportunity to participate in setting direction and making decisions that affect the enterprise, including information technology, human resources, and corporate services. Ensures those activities and decisions are aligned and the enterprise value of the investments is realized.

(continued)

Table 7.5 (*continued*)

Company	Forum	Function
PepsiCo	President's council includes all regional operating unit presidents and global category presidents, one level below executive committee. Marketing council is made up of global and regional marketing heads.	Reviews companywide portfolio of growth proposals from global category teams in a series of three meetings scheduled throughout the year. Provides connection between growth goals, brand and innovation initiatives, and regional operating plans, with one prioritized set of initiatives. Governs marketing policy, practice, and prioritizes key initiatives, in lieu of CMO position.
Rolls Royce— "Operating Committee"	Group leadership team meets monthly, and in addition to the five members on the executive board, it has an additional 12 members representing business units, geographies, and functions (e.g., HR, nuclear, marine, Germany, etc.).	Provides input and advice to the executive board on policy and strategy, discusses group performance, and serves as an important communication forum.

Some companies spend a great deal of time and energy filling in decision-rights templates, using RACI, RAPID, DICE, DAI, and other clever tools. The impact of these exercises is often disappointing. The tools are often confusing with debates regarding the definition of accountability, authority, and responsibility. They are used too broadly to capture activities, rather than decisions, creating fatigue and diffusing focus. They are often too simplistic when applied to complex decisions. Rather, we have found three keys to creating effective decision rights across a large company:

1. focus on a handful of high-value decisions that need more clarity.

2. understand the relationships that need to be built, and fit the tool or process to the relationship.

3. engage leaders across the company in learning how to make it work.

Focus on a handful of high-value decisions. Once the success targets are aligned between the various partners in the handshake and there is clear performance visibility for joint business results, clarifying decision rights is a logical next step. Most decisions do not require guidance when it comes to "who's got the D." Most are clear and are embedded in roles. Do not waste time building out RACI charts for those. The focus should be on the highest-value decisions that generate 80 percent of the tension. This should be a short list. Do not try to set rules that eliminate the need for tensions to play out; insist that the partners engage in conflict and debate on the important items in the handshake. Set practices that expect collaboration but drive speed. Be clear what a good decision looks like, and put in place the mechanism for how to move forward when agreement cannot be reached.

In order to identify which decision areas to focus on, it is useful to begin with a definition of the roles of the global and the local players in the handshake. A simple process view of the work is useful. Figure 7.2 maps the high-level steps in developing a new medical device and taking it to market. This snapshot makes it easy to isolate the key tension points among the roles that must work together.

After more than two years working the first phase of its global operating model, Deere & Co. chose to simplify a complex set of RACI charts that had failed to gain traction out in the business units. A short list of tension areas and guiding principles emerged from a series of meetings with regional and global business leaders in Beijing; Sao Paulo; Moline, Ill.; and Mannheim, Germany. After a few rounds of edits, engaging more than 150 senior leaders, it was concluded

	Insight	Concept	Development	Commercialization	Execution	Post-Launch
Global	• Concept Champion • Identify Unmet Need: Problem to Solve • Market Trends / Forces • Link to Broader Strategy	• Business Case Toolkit • Make-vs.-Buy Assessment • Evidence Strategy • Customer Segmentation	• NPD Planning • Commercial Plan • Training Plan • Evidence Plan • Coordinate Global Assumptions	• Global Launch Kit • Launch Phasing Plan • Commercial Stewardship • Communication Plan	• KPI Dashboard • Cost Reduction Plan • Best Practice Sharing • Launch Support • Communication / PR	• Portfolio Optimization • Obsolescence Strategy • Pricing Strategy • Regional Support
Region	• Key Opinion Leader Insights • Regional Market Dynamics • Challenge & Tailor Global Insights & Needs	• Financial Forecasts • Align w/Regional Leadership • Channel Strategy	• Local Validation Labs • Align Commercial Plans • Forecasts • Regional Account Segmentation	• Training • Deploy Launch Kit • Local Registration Required • Distributor Mgt.	• Program Execution • Forecast Updates • Best Practice Sharing • Regional Promotion	• Execution of Global Plan • Local Support • Specialty Marketing • Scaling Programs
Country	• Local Market Intelligence & Key Opinion Leader Insights	• Market Development Opportunity • Risk Mitigation • Pilots / Validation	• Go-to-Market Plan • Market Dev. Plan • Pilots / Validation	• PACE • Pricing / Tender Management • Evidence Execution	• Forecast Updates • Demand Generation Program • Ongoing Training	• Sales Support • Country Level Execution • Ongoing Training

Figure 7.2 A view of the product development process for a global medical devices company.

that six key decision-making areas accounted for most of the decision confusion in the global-to-local handshakes:

1. Business target setting (strategic and annual)

2. New product offering and sourcing

3. Asset management—dealer inventory levels

4. Asset management—raw materials, work in process

5. Pricing

6. Staffing decisions

These became the focus for defining decision rights, eliminating a great deal of potential work. Additionally, the team determined that a set of decision principles could serve as effective broad guidance:

- Winning faster in the market with customers is the starting point for our decisions.

- Decisions should be pushed down to the lowest practical level, and decision makers will be accountable.

- On the rare occasion the parties cannot agree, one will have the golden vote; escalation to a higher level should be the last resort.

- Individuals decide, not committees.

- Once decisions are made, focus will be on execution.

Understand decision relationships and fit the tool. The type of partnership that underlies a decision helps determine what tools are most useful. We like Susan Finerty's framework of three kinds of partnerships that exist in global matrix organization: a) transactional, b) collaborative, and c) integrated as shown in Table 7.6 (Finerty 2012). *Transactional* partners are typified by a customer–provider relationship where one partner serves the other. These relationships are less about decision rights and more about setting mutual expectations for service. The *collaborative* partnership requires more give and take across the boundaries, and while collaboration is expected, here it is useful to identify decision rights when there is a conflict. Decision rights help

Table 7.6   Types of partnership in the matrix organization. (Adapted from S. Finerty.)

	Transactional (Customer/Provider)	Collaborative (Give and Take)	Integrated (Fully Interdependent)
Description	One role is clearly accountable to make a good decision, but is dependent upon others to provide service, data, insight, or technical advice.	Two or more roles are expected to make decisions together. When there is disagreement, roles collaborate, not compromise to find a better solution. When agreement cannot be reached, one role is given the "golden vote" to make the call. This role is accountable for the quality of the decision.	Two or more roles truly co-own and comanage business results.
Implications for Partners	• Don't spend time on decision rights here. • Focus on service level agreements, expectations and behaviors, measures of performance, and resource discussions.	• Making these decisions will become easier over time—they require common data, trust based on experience, and reflection and learning based on real outcomes. • Decision rights are useful to make expectations clear and keep the work moving.	• Tend to be decisions around strategy and big investments at the very heart of the business direction. • Simple decision rights don't work for these. Leadership needs to be aligned. • These are a small in number, but expect to spend a lot of management time here.
Examples of Decisions	Service levels a business needs from a support function	In-market pricing and promotion strategy	Investment in a new customer segment across a set of markets

to increase speed and make clear that one party is ultimately accountable for the quality of the decision. The needs of both partners are important, and clear contracting of roles and alignment of objectives is required.

The *integrated* partnership is one of full interdependence. In this relationship the goals are shared completely. The partners co-own the customer and/or the consumer, they coauthor strategy, and they co-own the results. Integrated decisions don't lend themselves to simplistic tools.

Collaborative business issues lend themselves well to tools like RACI and DICE, as long as they are kept simple. In fact, we have a strong preference for reducing these to a binary tool that simply distinguishes who in the handshake gets the tipping vote on difficult issues when collaboration doesn't result in agreement. These partnerships are akin to a joint venture with a designated 51 percent and 49 percent partner. The best practice for decision rights is to designate who will act as the 51 percent partner for a given issue. For example, for product development decisions, the global business-unit leader in the Philips consumer lifestyle sector gets the 51 percent vote if agreement is not reached with the market. But on advertising and promotion decisions, the regional market leader gets the golden vote. We stress these high-value decisions require heavy collaboration, but when the partners cannot agree, speed requires the team to move on, trusting that the 51 percent partner (on that issue!) will make an informed call. In the binary decision chart example shown in Table 7.7, an X represents the 51 percent partner and the O represents the 49 percent partner.

For decisions about complex systems, investments in mega projects, or fundamental strategic direction, RACI and the binary (51/49 percent) partnership tools often will not work. They are too prescriptive and can force dangerous, overly simple answers to complex, high-risk situations. ConocoPhillips launched its global operating model in 2012 in an attempt to incorporate more sophisticated technical know-how, operational consistency, and robust risk management into its exploration and production operations around the world. Two years into this organizational change, the company embarked on an "organizational health check" in response to a series of mounting and largely unresolved tensions between the operators and the functional leaders. The cost structure was rising and the external pressure of falling oil prices made it difficult to ignore these issues.

Table 7.7   Decision-rights example for high-collaboration issues, defines "golden vote" 51 percent (X) and 49 percent (O) for global and regional partners in the handshake.

	Region Market Leader	Global Business Leader	Notes and Assumptions
Annual target setting	O	X	Collaborative Strategic plan, portfolio decision making in BU Annual target sets framework for resourcing, pricing, operating P&L
Resourcing	X	O	Commercial cost, part of joint plan, adjustments by region
P&L corrective actions	X	O	Region accountable for annual results
Strategic pricing	O	X	Shift to global business unit Regional pricing needed to manage cross-border differences, limit parallel trade, price spiral
Tactical pricing	X	O	Strategic pricing framework, corridor Region freedom to move within, with exceptions to group
Product portfolio	O	X	BU sets business case Market has role in escalating local portfolio changes to sector then executive committee
Advertising & promotion	X	O	Part of joint business plan Boundary set by strategic P&L and Chief Marketing Officer for local brand management

The organizational health check included in-depth interviews with the top 30 executives at ConocoPhillips. The stakes are high in oil and gas fields, with investment choices, technical and economic viability trade-offs, geopolitical risks, and environment and safety issues all to be considered. It is critical to achieve the right balance between operating unit autonomy and management of risk and technological excellence. The organizational health-check interviews revealed a handful of opportunities for greater alignment, mostly in the relationship between the Houston-based technology and exploration functions and the production operating units around the globe. The proliferation of functional initiatives during the previous two years, aimed at driving more operational consistency, productivity, and safety, had reached a level that caused the operators to feel overwhelmed with dictates and resource-consuming programs. Unresolved power issues between the center and the operating units made it difficult to problem solve tension areas. A lack of trust and candor confounded the problems, sometime leading to passive resistant behaviors. Efforts to use RACI-type tools did not work for these major issues, the ones that most needed attention.

Finerty's three partnership types (transactional, collaborative, and integrated) provided an excellent framework for handshake conversations between operating units and functions. All three of these partnership types are in play in the oil fields. The task was to focus on those to the far right, in the integrated partner column of Table 7.6, those that required a very different kind of conversation among the players.

When drilling technologists work with a local field operation, the two must work in an integrated fashion, along with project management, financial, and other technology players. To codify expectations, a team of operating GMs and technology function heads sat together to identify a set of scenarios that typified these highly integrated partnership challenges. Each one-page scenario spelled out an issue, the players, the points of tension, and the kinds of conversations and behavior needed to manage the tension area. Research into major programs that had been less than completely effective revealed the need for candor and openness, and the benefits of deep, cross-functional analysis of the issues before moving ahead. Business units that chose to keep technical resources at arm's length in the interest of speed and autonomy did not do as well as those that fully engaged with available resources. By the same token, functions that tended to push mandates without engaging their general management colleagues got less traction from their efforts. These insights led to drafting a set of principles, and each applied to the various tension scenarios that had been documented. (See Table 7.8.)

Table 7.8   Decision principles at ConocoPhillips.

1. Start with the right conversation.

2. Keep mandates few and engage partners.

3. Make certain standards are fit for purpose.

4. Opt out of technical support with care.

5. Put your cards on the table.

6. Go slow to go fast.

7. Escalate real concerns.

These contracted agreements provide considerable guidance, but they do rely a great deal on the emotional intelligence and agility of the team members, as we will see in the next chapter of the book.

Engage leaders across the company in learning how to make it work. Documenting expectations is one thing, but winning buy-in and helping leaders know what to do is another. Successful efforts to establish clear guidance for decision making nearly always include high degrees of leadership enrollment in the process. There are at least three sets of tactics that can help to activate decision rights:

1. Involve a cross-section of the affected leadership in identifying tension scenarios and developing solutions to manage them (this is a powerful action research opportunity that should be supported by human resources).

2. Integrate the scenarios and the decision-rights outputs into leadership conferences and leader development programs (make it part of the standing curriculum, key messages, and stories that are told by leaders).

3. Establish clear expectations that effective boundary-spanning behaviors are prerequisites for advancement to senior positions in the business.

Designing effective decision-making processes and relationships into the global operating model may be the most challenging task in the activation process. Activation is dependent upon the decision velocity of an organization. One of the reasons that activation takes time, often years, is that some high-value decisions are only made once or a few times in a year. Making them in new forums, with new processes, and new mindsets—and then reflecting and evaluating on the quality of the outcome and adjusting—can only happen as often as the decisions need to be made. Attending to the balance of power and building productive governance forums and healthy decision partnerships takes sustained effort. Executive teams should not ignore or shortcut this important work.

SUMMARY OF THE CHAPTER

- Power for purpose should be designed into global operating models, rather than relying on historic patterns of authority and influence, or settling for political resolution.

- Vertical power arrangements define delegation down into the organization; horizontal power arrangements define how peer groups in the matrix make decisions.

- Relative power relationships between global and local business units can and should be adjusted consciously with changes in reporting relationships, budget controls, decision authority, and the nature of talent placed into positions.

- Each company needs to find its own unique formula for balancing the global and the local agenda and decision authority. This includes redefining country and market manager roles and their authority with regard to local market development, customer management, public affairs, business services, and talent scouting.

- Top leadership should define the nature of the desired operating governance in the company and clarify the roles of governing forums, including executive and operating committees, portfolio committees, key councils, and the like.

- Decision rights can be a very useful part of activating the global operating model, but the tools should be fit for purpose, as simple as possible, and should engage a cross section of leadership in aligning around the conclusions.

PART III

THE RIGHT BEHAVIOR AND KNOW-HOW

The studies on the successes and failures of corporate transformations are not very encouraging. One of the more comprehensive studies indicates that only about one-third of enterprise change initiatives achieve any success at all (McGuire and Rhodes 2009). A failure to change the leadership know-how and mindset is often the breakdown in less successful initiatives.

While the right connections and the right conversations are critical to bringing a global organization to life, no amount of process, decision rights, management routines, and well-wired networks can overcome weak relationships and leadership behaviors that destroy value for the enterprise. As intuitive as this is, and as often as we hear the argument from operators that great talent is more important than the right organization structure, still somehow the leadership talent gap persists. There are many reasons, including the unwillingness of top leaders to make hard choices on talent. Of course, staffing choices are more difficult and more troubling when the global talent bench is thin.

Eighteen months into the activation of its global category-focused transformation, Nike's top leadership decided to accelerate the change process by moving some of its highest potential executives out of senior product management and commercial management roles into the new global category positions. The impact of this staffing change was dramatic in shifting the cultural center of gravity from product and regional sales to consumer-focused categories. The effect of landing heavyweights in these new positions was partially symbolic, but because these new players were collaborative, agile leaders who had worked and lived in international environments, they built extended teams made up of other talented people, and quick wins were usually not far behind.

Chapter 8 explores the nature of global leadership in the horizontal organization. We attempt to capture fresh and usable insight from decades of research on global leadership competencies. We take a close look at the talent management systems and practices in companies that are known for producing a deep talent pipeline, especially the purposeful use of experience-based strategies and learning programs that make organization design part of the management development process.

CHAPTER 8

Matrix-Ready Leaders

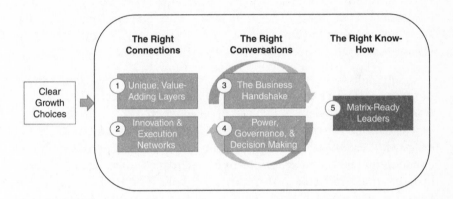

In 1990 C.K. Prahalad wrote an article titled "Globalization: The Intellectual and Managerial Challenges." In this paper he described the future global environment for business leaders.

> *A world where variety, complex interaction patterns among various subunits, host governments, and customers, pressures for change and stability, and the need to reassert individual identity in a complex web of organizational relationships are the norm. This world is beset with ambiguity and stress. Facts, emotions, anxieties, power and dependence, competition and collaboration, individual and team efforts are all present. (Prahalad 1990)*

Prahalad was a visionary to be sure; 25 years later, no one has captured the global leadership challenge more effectively.

The matrix that underlies a global operating model requires strong leaders who can manage multiple teams, influence peers without authority, and proactively align competing agendas. The success of a global operating model depends largely on competent leaders who are willing and able to navigate the power dynamics inherent in a complex organization.

THE HORIZONTAL LEADERSHIP MANDATE

"Today the leadership advantage goes to the people who are most closely linked to others and can work with a great variety of people from differing positions, backgrounds, and locations" (Ernst and Chrobot-Mason 2011). This conclusion emerged from an expansive study by the Center for Creative Leadership (CCL) on managing across geographic, functional, demographic, and other boundaries.

One hundred years of management science have delivered plenty of theory and practice in how to lead a hierarchical (vertical) organization. But our thinking is much less evolved when it comes to leadership in a horizontal organization. In the CCL study 71 percent of the managers who responded indicated that horizontal leadership was the most challenging task, compared with only 7 percent who indicated vertical leadership was difficult in their organizations. The CCL definition of lateral leadership works for us: "Boundary spanning leadership is the ability to create direction, alignment, and commitment across boundaries in service of a higher vision or goal."

Tim Shriver is the longtime chairman of Special Olympics International and the son of its founder, Eunice Kennedy Shriver. He recently passed the CEO role to a successor, and during the search process he reflected on the success formula for leadership in a global nonprofit like Special Olympics. Leadership in a far-flung volunteer organization is instructive for business leaders who want to be effective in the lateral organization. If you sit in the center, your ability to influence managers out in the regional market teams can be very much like working with a volunteer organization—when it is working right. Take a look at Shriver's point of view and consider the relevant parallels to the corporate world.

> We are very aware of the need to be global and local. I'm a bit of a student of the Catholic Church in this matter. How do you create something that is completely embedded locally and at the same time is universal and makes people feel part of the whole? The mission is the core to creating universal relevance, and there

are tough challenges in the developing world. You have to answer questions like, how do we tap into the spirit of human dignity in Egypt and Libya and not use language that will get us in trouble in China?

The beauty of the model is that everyone in the organization looks down the chain to feel accountable—ultimately to the Special Olympics athlete. Coaches, program directors, and regional heads—everyone looks to the athlete to determine are we doing it right. We can't directly motivate volunteers but we can create a culture that shapes volunteer behavior—rooted in the mission. There is a mix needed between the right stuff, the belief in the movement, and the right experience and training. It starts with the passion—with belief in what you're doing. Empowerment is a big part of it. We are religiously nonhierarchical. *(Kesler 2011)*

A COMPETENCY-BASED VIEW OF GLOBAL LEADERSHIP

In our work with global companies, we have viewed the leadership challenge through an organization transformation lens, and have learned a great deal about the kind of leaders and leadership development practices that are fundamental to activating the global operating model. The first place to start is with the talent, skills, and know-how necessary for leaders today.

Leadership has become a major field of study, and the proliferation of competency models over the past 30 years is staggering, including models that are specific to the global business context. Unfortunately, most of the studies that produced myriad competency frameworks were conducted separately, rarely building on each other, and often motivated by proprietary control of the content for commercial purposes.

Mark Mendenhall, of the University of Tennessee, conducted an exhaustive review in 2013 of the literature on global leadership competencies (Mendenhall et al. 2013). The authors of this impressive study make the case that the global context changes leadership skill requirements not only in degree, but in kind. Living and working in the global context with its intensity of complexity often creates a transformational experience for jobholders. Warren Bennis argued that these experiences act as development crucibles to produce new mental models, new worldviews, and perspectives unique to those who have had the experience (Bennis and Thomas 2002). In many ways, global leadership means unlearning much of what made one successful in a domestic leadership career.

Mendenhall and his colleagues reviewed 160 competency models in order to consolidate the research. They were able to sort them into a handful of competency categories, which allowed them to distinguish among personal traits, knowledge, and behavioral skills. Essentially, the framework argues, all competency dimensions are rooted in three broad domains, referred to as the global leadership triad (Brake 1997; Bird 2013):

1. business and organization acumen (cognitive traits, knowledge and skills);

2. managing people and relationships (sensitivity traits and skills); and

3. managing self (self-awareness and other personal traits, enhanced by experience).

Building on this understanding of competency work, two of the scholars in this study developed an integrated view of global leadership competencies, known as the pyramid model of global leadership, as shown in Figure 8.1 (Bird and Osland 2013).

We believe the pyramid model of global leadership is the best summary we have seen of a complex topic. It is most useful to examine the dimensions from an application point of view—that is, how a company might put them to work. Some competency dimensions are rooted in personal traits that are hardwired in nature, while others are more easily developed through the right experiences and exposure to knowledge and skill building (Lombardo and Eichinger 2002). It follows naturally then that companies should hire for the hardwired traits and then concentrate on developing those qualities that can be shaped through learning, coaching, and experience. The seven key dimensions, from the pyramid, that we think are most critical to activating a global operating model are described below.

Competencies to hire for:

- Inquisitiveness
- Cognitive complexity
- Building trust

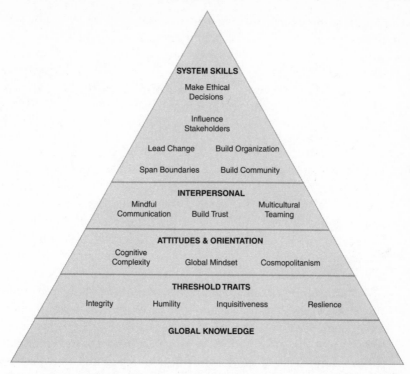

Figure 8.1 Pyramid model of global leadership by Bird and Osland.

Competencies to develop:

- Influencing stakeholders
- Global mindset
- Build organization
- Build community

Inquisitiveness (organizational curiosity and learning agility). This characteristic is the desire to have new experiences and to learn from them. It is the innate interest in business dynamics and curiosity as to how other parts of the company make money. It is the basis for authentic and sincere working relationships, where colleagues seek to understand the objectives and challenges they each face. Learning agility is a well-documented factor for measuring leadership potential (Lombardo and Eichinger 2004). Global leaders who score well on this trait are quick to sign up for unusual assignments that involve uncertainty and ill-defined responsibilities, often in parts of the world where it can be very difficult to do business. They find a way to succeed and they learn from the experience. The research says those with high learning agility learn faster, not because they are more intelligent, but because they have more effective learning skills and attitudes. This is often a proxy for potential because it is clear that a healthy measure of this trait undergirds other competencies (Black et al. 1999).

Cognitive complexity (systems thinking, able to conceptualize the whole, and manage trade-offs). This factor is the ability of a leader to see the many elements of the system around them and the relationships among those elements. It allows them to see the discrete market segments, tactics, capabilities, and objectives in a business strategy, and to see how they all must fit together to achieve overall company results. Leaders who are high in this quality are able to work through the tensions of global versus local objectives and short versus long term. Leaders we have worked with in client companies, who have grown up in places like P&G and Unilever, often stand out among their peers as the most comfortable with the seeming chaos of the transformation to a global matrix. They are not thrown by the complexity of the multidimensional strategy and model or the myriad relationships and agendas that must be juggled.

Build trust (integrity, humility, courage). This is a behavioral factor, rooted in personal characteristics of integrity and humility. Relationships and social capital are the coin for getting things done in the matrix organization. No amount of business process, handshakes, or alignment of reward systems is likely to overcome poor relationships among international colleagues. When trust is low (and tensions are high), many destructive behaviors follow, including the need people feel to attend all meetings and fight battles over every point of disagreement, out of fear that counterparts in the matrix will not act with their best interests in mind. Trust is also the foundation of delegation and empowerment. There is no substitute for leaders who value trusting relationships, know how to build them, and actively do so. Communicating with courage is also important in the matrix. Courage is required to advocate for unpopular views with peers and managers. It also refers to how well one receives bad news or failure. We have observed with a number of client companies that, despite stated values to the contrary, there is a "high cost of candor."

Influence stakeholders (sell compelling ideas across boundaries). This is a universal factor for leadership, but the number and the diversity of peer stakeholders is higher in the global matrix. Direct authority is impossible in global partnerships, even when decision rights are relatively clear. Leadership is shared and may even rotate from one team member to another during the innovation cycle. Externally, global managers must be influential with innovation partners, foreign governments, and the public. Western companies that want influence in the business community in China carefully select high-influence leaders who bring compelling ideas built on deep knowledge of the marketplace. Influence is a skill that can be learned, often by holding jobs with considerable responsibility but limited authority, such as staff roles and major project management assignments.

Global mindset (true appreciation for the value of differences). Leaders with a true global mindset see the world beyond the borders of their own homeland and culture. This one may be among the more difficult to operationalize, but it shows up in the way candidates view the world and their tendency to fall victim to the biases of culture. US-bred leaders who rely on "Americanisms" to communicate often struggle to make themselves understood, never mind trusted. Commercial leaders with a global mindset do not default to assumptions from their own markets when they consider brand or product possibilities. Again, hardwired traits of curiosity tend to make this one easier to develop, but living outside one's home country and having to find your way around a different culture is the only way to gain this mindset.

Build community (align agendas and create networks). Global leaders have to build communities across product, function, and regional teams that may have not always have aligned views. The business-market handshake is one of those communities. Center-based marketing and product leaders who build tight docking points between their own teams and regional marketers view the players out in the markets as members of the same community regardless of reporting relationship. R&D staff in those same regions deliver faster, more aligned results when they feel they are a part of that community. The highest form of community building happens when the leader is able to get the diverse players to shift identity from their own country-based unit to a global brand in which they have a stake and a voice. Many function leaders believe that they need all functional staff to report to them in order to run a global function. Certainly, this visibility and control makes resource allocation easier. However, we have seen many global functional leaders who directly control very little exert tremendous influence by actively building a strong professional identity and community around the world.

Organization architecting (configure and continually improve structure and process). This is a skill, and a relatively advanced one, that is critical for senior leaders in the global matrix. We believe that senior leaders across the matrix need to understand the basic principles of organization design, the star model, and the relationships among the star points. Understanding the organization as a system and how various actions will impact behavior and outcomes in the system is fundamental to leading in a complex organization. Even more important is for senior leaders to have a common vocabulary and set of organizational frameworks so that they can work together to make activation decisions and communicate with their teams with one voice.

BUILDING A GLOBAL LEADERSHIP TALENT PIPELINE

One of the interesting markers of a company that has pushed the global operating model forward over time is the number of multinationals in the c-suite. The CEO at The Coca-Cola Co. is the third non-American in a row in the assignment (an Australian, an Irish-born South African, and now a Turkish national). Not to be outdone in the global cola talent wars, PepsiCo's long-sitting CEO is an American-naturalized woman, born in India. The c-suites in both these companies have recently included citizens of Cameroon, France, Sudan, Ireland, Turkey, U.K., Nigeria, and India. The top seven line executives at Coca-Cola today come from six different countries. Both of these companies are well regarded for their global talent practices, and in both cases these practices are rooted in insights derived from the careers of the sitting leaders, many of whom held a series of diverse and stretch international assignments.

Interestingly, the broad base of international talent in the Coke system is made up largely of graduates of a global staffing campaign initiated by former CEO Doug Ivester in the mid-1990s. Ivester sponsored an aggressive campaign for global general management talent that led to the hiring of 100 external multinational players. Some were placed in significant jobs, and others went through a series of lateral assignments in middle management. Over the following five years or so, perhaps as many as half left the company, but those who stayed became the core of a robust global talent pool, from which nearly all of today's top executives have been groomed and promoted. That initiative is now 20 years old. Building a global talent pipeline is not a quickly accomplished initiative.

Korn Ferry's Kent DeMeuse and colleagues refer to this kind of staffing approach as geocentric, when candidates for headquarters and local roles are drawn from an international talent pool (DeMeuse et al. 2009). In contrast, an ethnocentric approach refers to a staffing process where key positions are filled by parent-country nationals, often from the corporate headquarters. In between these extremes, the polycentric staffing model is utilized when foreign subsidiaries are staffed primarily by host-country nationals from the subsidiary locations. A conscious mix of these staffing models is a good place to start a talent strategy, based on a deep, fact-based analysis of the current talent pool.

Assessment data regarding the existing pool of players should be part of the organizational transformation process. We have previously referenced studies on common staffing errors that place legacy leadership skills into substantially new roles (CLC 2010). Filling key gaps in the leadership pipeline may be difficult during restructuring, but these are also golden moments of opportunity that should not be missed.

Building a global talent pipeline is a core capability for companies that want to activate a global operating model. Clear talent objectives drive the right talent development focus. P&G provides a good example. Senior leader target positions come broadly in three forms: a) global business units, b) market development regions, and c) functions and services. Talent depth is measured in each track, and strategies are built to strengthen projected gaps.

TALENT + EXPERIENCE = THE RIGHT STUFF

We have borrowed the header for this section from researchers Bird and Osland, who provide an excellent summary of the research on experience-based development (Bird and Osland 2013). The benefits of actively managing experience-based development are well documented, and Chief Human Resource Officers (CHROs) know it works. But not just any experience works to develop high-potential leaders. Bird and Osland found that the nature of the experience determined its impact on development, and the likelihood leaders would assume greater responsibility depends upon: a) complexity, b) intensity, c) emotional impact, and d) relevance.

Complexity. The greater the challenges in a role or project, the more a leader's ability to manage complexity is tested and developed. Complexity comes in different forms. Often tasks that may be of moderate complexity in the home country are more complex in the international environment. Executing what are simple logistics in some places, such as distributing soft drinks across a country, can be very challenging and complex in Nigeria, where the general manager may have to resolve trade barriers, currency issues, and security and transportation in remote areas. Contrast that kind of complexity with solving sophisticated marketing problems in very saturated and mature consumer markets in Western Europe or North America. Some companies differentiate these forms of complexity and encourage future senior leaders to have both kinds of experiences.

Intensity. Initiatives that require concentrated attention and effort, such as leading a very challenging turnaround project against a tough deadline in an international environment, provide intense experiences. High degrees of intensity increase the likelihood that learning is retained and that pattern recognition is developed. In helping to activate large-scale organizational changes, we have worked with a number of high-potential middle managers in project leadership roles over 6- to 12-month periods of time. These can be very intense assignments, and the players walk away with a far more sophisticated understanding of organizational dynamics in large corporations than they would get in the normal course of business.

Emotional impact. Experiences that stimulate deep emotional responses—frustration, anxiety, and elation, for example—are absorbed in a manner that makes vivid recall more likely. These unforgettable experiences may be revisited over the course of a person's career. Setbacks, even getting fired, are among those experiences. One's first offshore assignment can have emotional impact over an entire career, especially living in developing countries.

Relevance. This is a more subjective factor and can only be measured by the incumbent. The more that leaders believe an experience is relevant to their future objectives, the more likely they will ascribe importance to it, leading to greater impact. This is largely influenced by culture and messaging from the top of the organization. The more it is expected that high potentials take lateral assignments and live overseas, the higher the motivation to take on these challenges and the higher the learning.

P&G has considered these factors and has formalized development experience paths accordingly. There are three critical experiences that any future senior general manager at P&G must have:

1. manage multiple brands in a single country;

2. manage a single business around the world; and

3. a job living in a foreign country.

Lateral moves are expected in this culture. Additionally, leadership development is linked to P&G's core capabilities. Consumer insights and innovation are fundamental areas of expertise that general managers are expected to develop through the right jobs, supplemented with the right education and training (Lafley and Martin 2013).

DEVELOPING LEADERS AND ORGANIZATION AT THE SAME TIME

The best global leadership systems develop people and the organization simultaneously (Tichy et al. 1992). No other business process has more impact on shaping culture than companywide talent development forums. Calibration and development councils can become the control centers for activation if used well. As an executive team at the top does the work of getting to know its talent by evaluating players with a common yardstick and vocabulary, they begin to calibrate a shared set of expectations about what global leadership looks like in their company. As they plan chess moves among promotable candidates, they learn to trust and they play more of an enterprise leadership role, often becoming a more collaborative leadership team. For many companies this new organization model shifts the roles of senior executives from fully focused on the performance of their own unit, to committing a portion of their attention to shared leadership of the enterprise. By investing in the talent conversation, they are "being the change," working together with behaviors that *are* the global operating model.

Neville Isdell was called back from retirement in 2004 to be the CEO of Coca-Cola, to guide what turned out to be a major turnaround in the company's fortunes. Among the handful of levers that Isdell focused on first was a refreshed talent review process, centered on driving dialogue, calibration, and planned development moves against a new set of leadership criteria (Kesler 2008). Isdell and his newly formed leadership team worked together by first exposing themselves to rigorous assessments of their own leadership strengths and gaps. The assessments were completed against a new set of competencies and linked to five enterprise capabilities in the company's new "manifesto for growth." Isdell made it a constructive, positive process that filled a gap of many years during which there had been little or no feedback to leaders about their development opportunities. Some of the executives who had been brought into the company through Ivester's future general management sourcing program, called the general management talent initiative (GMTI) were elevated to big jobs. Talent forums were later launched across the organization for all major operating units and functions; formal assessment-center styled workshops were held around the globe in search of the next generation of general managers, and many of the general managers from GMTI acted as assessors of this next generation of talent.

Executive teams soon discover the power is in the dialogue—the conversation, not the tools. Bill Conaty, retired CHRO from GE, makes the case that business outcomes are the result of a social process working at every level, inside and outside the company. Breakthroughs in talent management happen when you connect talent management into the social process as well as the business process (Conaty and Charan 2010).

New norms are established through conversations about the performance and potential of the leadership bench. One of the first tests is how candid executives choose to be in discussing the relative strengths of their direct reports and other key players. Few other conversations are more loaded with trust issues. The tendency often is for talent reviews to be staged presentations. Peers avoid candid sharing of views about individuals and may hide and hoard key talent from others. In a well-facilitated talent process these norms are challenged, and trust gradually increases.

As the new organization model emerged at Coke, talent and organization comingled, in a healthy way, as the executive team began reconsidering the scale and the scope of division general management jobs out in the regions, and the collaboration that would be necessary with global brand leader roles in Atlanta. The profile for successful leadership adjusts as the new organization model comes into greater focus. Talent movement acts as a weaving process in the matrix, creating a talent pool of players who understand what life is like in the center, in the field, and in staff and as well line positions.

LEARNING PROGRAMS AND CULTURE CHANGE

Learning programs can play a major role in developing leaders, especially in the midst of a transition to a new, global operating model. People need to understand the new organizational intentions and to be assured that the challenges they are experiencing are completely normal and expected. Further, when education and awareness are combined with skill building and the opportunity to successfully cocreate with new colleagues, managers are more open to taking personal risks to change behavior and invest in high-trust relationships. When these three kinds of learning are woven together, they have the simultaneous effect of developing the organization and its leaders: a) the fundamentals of matrix logic, b) building trusting relationships and networks, and c) activating the right operating mechanisms. Such learning is best delivered as case-based, action-learning workshops that are aimed at developing individuals, teams, and the greater organization. Each session delivers outputs that go into the change management plan.

The fundamentals of matrix logic. Learning to lead in the matrix starts with understanding some of the principles we have laid out in this book. It is often a revelation to managers to learn that the tension felt in the matrix organization is there for a reason, and that the goal is not to eliminate that tension, but to use it to extract the most value from the business. We often build this content into design sessions early in the change process, and continue to build on the messages through the activation process. In companies that have already implemented a new organization, this material is often introduced through an after-action review to continue to develop leaders to be more effective. GE, Intel, Levi's, QVC, and others have embedded this content into their management development curriculum.

Building trusting relationships and networks. Managers in all the companies we have worked with are eager to talk about relationships. During our organizational assessments, we frequently hear managers characterize their organization culture as one that values being nice at the expense of debate. As a result, decisions are made without visibility to the strategic rationale. The global operating model thrives on straight talk, and those who speak truth to power have to be valued and reinforced.

Relationship building is not only a matter of working across national and ethnic cultures, but also across departmental ones. Finance executives speak a distinct language and behave based on distinct business values and perspectives, and so do marketers, and engineers, and scientists. "Microcultures" are very real barriers to establishing trust and understanding (Shell and Moussa 2008).

In the large petroleum company that we discussed earlier, once an organizational health check had identified improvement areas (after two years into the new global formation) teams were asked to identify ways to improve effectiveness. One team, focused on the trust and candor issue, conducted interviews and a survey to understand how leaders perceived a) the level of candor among the top 125 executives, b) the impact of lack of candor, and c) the barriers to greater trust. Indeed, the trust and candor gap was assessed to be high. The perceived consequences of a lack of candor included avoidance of performance problems, unwillingness to challenge others' priorities, and reluctance to set stretch targets. Among the perceived barriers was the finding that when these issues were raised to higher management they tended to be downplayed, and that to be candid was likely to lead to a label of being noncollaborative. These survey results were brought back to the extended leadership team in a facilitated session. The survey data were mixed into a workshop with a simple trust model, examples of how best practice companies manage conflict in the matrix, and interactive breakout sessions. The CEO and his team participated fully and were prepared to openly welcome the conversation. This would be the first of several discussions, but these new conversations signaled real change.

Activating the right operating mechanisms. Management workshops with a cross section of leaders from around the world are the very best way to define decision rights and bring them to life. Early in the design work managers will make assumptions regarding how points of tension will be resolved, but real decision clarity work often can't take place until the people are in new roles and have started to work and make decisions together. In this way, decision rights are based on the real high-value/high-risk scenarios that matter to managers in the business. The frameworks and tools described in Chapter 7 can be used to identify idea outcomes to these scenarios. These scenarios then become stories built into communication and on-boarding materials.

Quest Diagnostics held a top 200 leadership conference to launch its enterprise-wide reorganization in 2012. Breakout sessions were focused on collaborative P&L handshakes between regional commercial units and a new set of franchise business units. The handshake model was presented, and intact regional teams met with franchise leaders in breakout sessions to prioritize what products and services were most important to growth in a given region, followed by ranking of initiatives and identifying the most critical targets for interlock between business units and regional teams. Such sessions get people started working productively across boundaries.

Change is social process. That is what makes large-group design and activation sessions so powerful. Dick Axelrod and Marv Weisbord have both developed methodologies for "getting the entire system in the room" to drive major change initiatives (Axelrod and Block 2010; Weisbord and Janoff 2010). High participation methods have influenced our practice, and we have previously written about the "design charette," a large-group design session that engages from 25 to 150 people in an intense two-day design event (Kesler and Kates 2011). We strongly endorse bringing together a large cross section of leaders made up of players from multiple businesses, functions, and geographies to align around the case for change, to interact with top executives, and to work in small groups to detail the new organizational framework. Once the core design is complete, the circle of participation is broadened to define decision rights, work on process improvements, and align objectives. The outcome of this engagement is a better design and a critical mass of change agents unleashed into the business. These sessions produce a bottom-up momentum for transformation that is very difficult to turn back. They are also action-learning events that prepare leaders to work effectively in the matrix.

THE ROLE OF TOP EXECUTIVES

As obvious as it may sound, top executives must lead by example to activate the global operating model. Without alignment at the top this is impossible to do. It takes courage for the chief executive to confront executives who agree to change in meetings, but don't back up their words with action. If the senior operating executives in a company that seeks more integration of the operating model continue to believe that they can only be successful with high degrees of autonomy, the dynamics of the executive team tend to devolve to "I won't interfere with your business if you don't interfere with mine." What is needed instead are strong business leaders who can also comfortably wear an enterprise hat and help the CEO make trade-offs that are in the best interests of the company overall. A concrete example is the active management of the company-wide innovation and investment portfolio for a company seeking to become more integrated. It is a significant change of culture in highly decentralized companies for the executive team to dig deeply into the investment options for one another's business, evaluating the value of different options against an enterprise set of criteria.

The culture of an executive team can be measured. One cultural framework that helps to define the nature of the executive team and to align it with the new organization model defines three cultural types (McGuire and Rhodes 2009):

1. *Dependent-Conformer*—leadership is for those at the top. Success depends on hierarchy, loyalty, and control.

2. *Independent-Achiever*—leadership is distributed down into the organization, and there is a high expectation for individual responsibility, even competition, where company results are largely the sum of individual achievements.

3. *Interdependent-Collaborator*—leadership is shared both vertically and horizontally, where synergies are expected and the company's assets can only be productive with degrees of collaboration across businesses and functions.

After reading this book, we would expect few leaders to choose the first path of *dependent-conformer* as a way to competitive advantage. But the other two archetypes are genuine options. A sleepy giant that is trying to shake up its culture, with little expectation for collaboration or synergies across a diverse portfolio of businesses, might well choose the *independent-achiever* model for its executive culture. Companies that are privately held, have grown under a strong founder, or have had an easy path to past growth but are facing new performance imperatives often focus on stimulating individual achievement. If, on the other hand, the strategy calls for more integration across the businesses, the *interdependent-collaborator* culture should be the goal. A candid conversation about the existing leadership culture needs to happen to bring the top team into alignment.

Some of our client companies choose to gather upward feedback on the individual executives at the top of the house to help them be more effective in modeling the right behaviors. This is a very constructive thing to do that sends the message we all need to be part of the change. A review of middle management feedback to senior executives in our work over the last five years reveals a handful of common requests:

1. Help us align priorities.

2. Help us make the right trade-offs between decisiveness and collaboration.

3. Hold the new organizations accountable for the right results.

4. Model effective delegation and trust.

5. Treat conflicts as teaching moments.

Table 8.1 provides examples of the kind of comments that give rise to these themes, as well as some of the things executives can do to address them. As always, there are contradictions in the feedback. Most common, perhaps, is the tendency for middle management to want senior management to set clear direction and priorities while, at the same time, providing empowerment. The senior executive team needs to anticipate these contradictions and stay a consistent course in the messages that their behaviors send, while keeping their ears open.

A global operating model is only an aspiration until senior leadership activates it through collective and individual actions.

■ ■ ■

Table 8.1 Common feedback themes for senior executive behaviors

Themes	What Executives Can Do	Typical Comments from Managers
Help us align priorities.	Be certain the business strategy is clear. Set priorities that enable partners in the matrix to have a consistent view of the challenge. Be aware of the horizontal impact of decisions and behaviors that are not consistent with the strategy. Reach out to peers to solve horizontal disconnects that affect those who work for you.	"Alignment is critical. When you look at strategies from top to bottom, you have to be sure that the priorities are consistent all the way down to the operational level. Project M is a top-level competitive strategy, but when you get to the operational level, we start cancelling spending, and it creates a lot of confusion." "We have too many initiatives. It's constant and the field cannot absorb everything that is coming out from the center."
Help us make the right trade-offs between decisiveness and collaboration.	Encourage debate and ask the principals to work to resolve differences. Understand the benefit of investing time in joint decision making, but don't let the organization "swirl" too long. Make sure leaders learn from the experience.	"I would like to hear the division heads talk about what collaboration means, including conflict and what they really expect around consensus. Why not just say, we don't have to always agree. I'd like them to set the expectation that we don't always need a committee or full consensus. Let's define collaboration. The bias should be 'do something with it when it comes to you'."

Hold the new organization accountable for the right results.	Make sure certain metrics and incentives are aligned. Be consistent in holding both partners in the handshake accountable. Demand high performance in all key measures for both partners, and manage consequences consistently.	"The fact is, we are are very tough on the financials but we are very soft on how you get there in measuring customer performance, project execution, market share, and other operating measures. There are customer metrics, but there are no real consequences for those." "Our top leaders act like the regional sales groups are the 'real' P&L. Our global groups are still second-class citizens in the new organization."
Role model delegation and trust.	Trust the partners in the handshake to deliver. Don't interfere unnecessarily—manage by exception. Role model trust in your peers to do the right thing.	"Our top leadership is on the leading edge of micromanagement—and they are all three part of that." "It's demoralizing when across-the-board cuts in spending happen after we have worked so hard to align resources against our highest growth opportunities."
Treat conflicts as teaching moments.	Ask questions to understand the source of unresolved tensions. Help problem solve, by drawing the players back to the vision and strategy of the business. Role model straight talk. Don't take away the tension until someone has learned something, and ask, "How will it be different next time?"	"Members of our global team have to go back and ask for permission before decisions can get made. The matrix is a very slow way to work." "It's clear we don't like candor here. There too many sacred cows that we don't want on the table." "We're a very good news organization. No one wants to bring bad news forward." "We have too many people in the functions who act like they're running the business."

Summary of the Chapter

- Horizontal leadership—the ability to influence people and events across boundaries—is critical to activating the global operating model, and it has become more challenging in complex, global organizations.

- Among the most critical competencies for selecting and developing global leaders are: inquisitiveness, cognitive complexity, building trust, influencing stakeholders, global mindset, spanning boundaries, organization building, and community building.

- Purposeful, lateral talent moves that deliver challenging experiences across business lines, geographies, and functions are critical to activating the global organization with a strong leadership pipeline.

- Global talent reviews and leadership development programs can play a powerful role in culture change, part of activating the global operating model. At the same time, engaging leaders in organization design can be a powerful development experience.

- Top executives must lead by example to activate the global operating model, by leading across business units. Enterprise leadership includes willingness to collectively oversee the company-wide innovation and investment portfolio.

- During activation of a new operating model, middle managers often seek more top executive involvement in aligning priorities, helping with trade-off decisions, clarifying accountability, improving delegation, and managing conflict.

CHAPTER 9

Design Process
for Activation

The design and activation of a global operating model is a major undertaking that deserves a well–thought-out process and project infrastructure that is likely to be in place for two or more years.

We are often invited to work with an executive team on a new organization design once their work on the growth strategy is complete. The CEO often has a design concept in mind, but wants assistance rendering it in the level of detail that will guide implementation. We are also frequently asked to come two years or more after the initial implementation of a new organization model to assess what is not working and advise on how to speed activation. These latter projects have proven to be some of the richest learning experiences because we are able to take a close, diagnostic look at what has worked and what has stalled or has not produced the outcomes that were expected in a new organization design.

This chapter shares some of the insights about the *process* of activation. We encapsulate the findings as if we were sitting with the CEO and the Chief Human Resources Officer (CHRO) of a company about to embark on the design and activation process.

SET A ROAD MAP WITH A REALISTIC VIEW
OF THE TIMEFRAME

We have previously written about the organization design process, outlining five key design milestones for plotting a course from business case development to implementation. The five-milestone process is scalable for very large organization design initiatives as well as smaller,

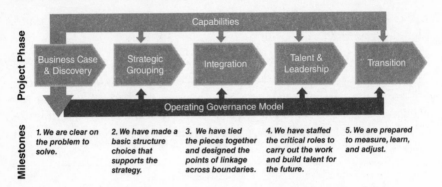

Figure 9.1   The five-milestone process for organization design.

subsystem designs (Kesler and Kates 2011). This model has provided a road map for a number of large system redesign initiatives. Each milestone is a decision point: a) a decision about a clear case for change; b) a decision on the basic strategic groups; c) a decision about how to integrate the groups; d) a decision about staffing new roles with the right talent; and, e) a decision about how to manage the transition. (See Figure 9.1.)

The framework can be used to blueprint the design process on a timeline. Of course, things are never as linear as the model suggests. Effective design work is iterative, but having a road map enables leadership to improvise where necessary without getting lost.

It is logical, then, to think about activation as a build on the final milestone—managing the transition—but that is too limited a view of activation. When the leadership team enters into the design process with a clear understanding of the activation imperative, the design work is managed all the way through the five milestones with an activation mindset. Activation is not something that happens at the end of the design process after implementation. Activation requires early engagement of the right players and robust design work on the "software" as well as the "hardware" for the new organization. Activation means culture change, and all the work of design teams and the communication campaign are lined up around consistent messaging about growth and the change that is required to achieve it.

The transition milestone in the model is where roles begin to shift, people change seats, new people are hired, and objectives and work assignments are realigned. Activation has already begun, and it will continue after the basic organization realignment has been completed, when the basics of implementation are done.

Taking a sustained approach to activation is not automatic. The urge to move on to the next set of opportunities is strong, and enthusiasm for the hard work of activation will wither if the CEO and the executive team don't stay actively involved. After the basic implementation is complete, management attention should be directed to a project plan that will bring the five activators to life.

Let's scan a typical set of activities that might be part of a robust activation project plan. These items are illustrative only, and the project plan for any one company could look very different. The point is that this work will not be completed in a few months and the scope and scale of it calls for a disciplined approach:

Unique Value-Adding Layers

- Set a plan for each business or region to remove layers where appropriate (by region or by business).

- Build out the plan for moving functional work up or down through organizational levels and/or to the shared services unit.

- Clearly define docking stations for global and regional points of contact.

- Set an execution plan for cost reductions.

- Communicate new role expectations clearly, with attention to how managerial roles and work mesh, up and down.

Innovation and Execution Networks

- Plan for business unit leaders to begin to work with regional teams to set shared priorities and roles for key initiatives in the network.

- Establish working practices and routines for each network.

- Define cross-functional communication practices, and begin to build cross-functional teams.

- Launch communities of practice with clear charters and build a learning plan.

- Set a plan for talent mix adjustments across the network.

Business Handshakes

- Launch handshake partnerships region by region and business by business.

- Agree on steps to set joint strategies and aligned objectives for each handshake.

- Set the metrics for each handshake with attention to collaborative profit and loss units, and develop dashboards for performance visibility.

- Establish new business review practices and routines.

- Define data requirements for the handshakes and begin to develop reporting mechanisms.

- Begin to develop core business processes (innovation, brand building, portfolio management).

Power, Governance, and Decision Making

- Plan transition to more integrated strategic planning, portfolio, and annual operating planning process.

- Clearly define roles and the operating cadence of key operating governance forums (executive committee, operating committee, councils, etc.). Be clear about how these groups interact and how they connect to the corporate calendar.

- Communicate role changes in key operating and functional positions to assure clear alignment and expectations.

- Begin to make adjustments in the power relationships between global and regional business units and functions (budget control, decision rights, portfolio oversight, etc.).

- Work through drafts of decision rights with the extended leadership team as part of learning and change management workshops.

Matrix-Ready Leaders

- Launch the new organization with the extended leadership team, and provide communication tools for driving messages throughout the organization.

- Assure that a talent strategy is in place for positions that have been substantially changed.

- Conduct workshops on leading in the matrix and building closer working relationships.

- Begin to implement changes in the global leadership talent pipeline process. Communicate new expectations for how the company will select and develop global leaders.

- Manage downsizing in a fashion that assures retention of best leaders.

- Assure that top executives role model the right behaviors throughout the activation process.

BUILD LEADERSHIP ALIGNMENT INTO THE PLAN

Let's start with the effects of poor alignment at the top. Messaging around major organizational changes is difficult under the best of circumstances. When there is lack of alignment on a clear case for change, the big idea behind the new organizational architecture tends to lose focus and may be remolded by the separate personalities on the executive committee. Over time, a once compelling idea for transforming a business can be lost among the many issues competing for management attention, especially when all the members of the top team are less than full owners of the case for change. Building a committed top team to help drive transformation starts with hard decisions about who has the ability and the willingness to make the journey.

Our work reveals natural resistance at the executive committee level to making major changes in the structure of business units, especially when it means diluting authority of general managers with matrixed or shared accountability. In contrast, the real voices for change, where the pain of the current working model is most apparent, are often one or two levels below the executive committee. This is one of the reasons that inclusion of these players is so important in the design process. The CEO and CHRO are smart to anticipate resistance from senior executive stakeholders and harness the energy for change at lower levels through a participative design process to create a "push upward."

In some past initiatives we have been assured by the CHRO that executive alignment will happen, that there is no need to build that into the plan because the CEO will make certain the team is aligned. Moving forward, with heads down, we have watched the misalignment emerge well into the design process. Often the CEO is uncomfortable confronting outlying executive committee members. These executives may be big revenue producers or have protective relationships with board members. As a result, passive resistance is often taken for buy-in. Lower-level design teams, meanwhile, are working hard on creating compelling visions of what could be only to see them rejected or ignored by members of the executive team who never had any intent of ceding power.

A better way starts with putting the cards on the table. Complete one-on-one interviews with executives, followed by facilitated, candid discussions about the findings. This helps the executive team move forward together toward a shared statement of the problem to solve. Candor and straight talk can be difficult among high-powered players in successful companies, but the view is worth the climb to alignment on the company's operating model. Without this alignment all further design and activation efforts will only end in frustration.

CEO leadership styles vary in terms of how direct the chief executive chooses to be in driving a change of this nature versus attempting to gain consensus, but it is impossible to gain alignment with the executive committee without a clear strong statement from the CEO regarding the global operating model. The impact of that story depends on the CEO's willingness to make the change personal, to engage others openly, and to call out successes as they happen. Plan to invest in team time at the top.

When Joe Almeida became the CEO of Covidien (formerly Tyco Healthcare, and now a large group within Medtronic) in 2011, he made a set of enterprise imperatives very clear to his new team. These imperatives spoke to a more integrated operating model than the company had utilized in the past with more leveraged resources, a more enterprise-wide view of the investment portfolio, and more interdependence between the global business units and the international regions. While he made these expectations clear, he also welcomed debate and wanted to know where his team stood. Interviews with each of his direct reports revealed two subgroups within his team, with very different perceptions of the nature of the existing operating model, much less any alignment on where the company should go. At a full day meeting only 30 days into Almeida's role as CEO, the differing views were discussed. He expressed an expectation that members would come together around his vision for the business, but he adjusted specifics based on feedback, and he conveyed confidence in the team. Over time some members of the team left the organization because they were not a good fit for the new operating model. Almeida remained tough-minded and very involved in bringing the new operating model to life, but he skillfully continued to build a climate of candor within the executive team. During the next two years, as business units were realigned to the new architecture, there were few surprises and little resistance from members of Covidien's leadership team. The company's performance was outstanding in the years following Almeida's transformation, and the subsequent merger with Medtronic was a big win for shareholders.

MANAGEMENT SUMMIT MEETINGS

We outlined in Chapter 7 the benefits of large-scale, "everyone in the room" design sessions. Alignment of the extended leadership team—with up to 100 or 200 members—is well served by this kind of participation. We often encourage companies that conduct an annual leadership conference to build the event into the project timeline. These sessions can be very effective as launch events that bring the extended leadership team into the activation process, once the design work and any restaffing is complete. The CEO and the executive committee have an opportunity to stand in front of the audience and demonstrate they are one team in driving the change forward. These are powerful symbolic opportunities not to be missed.

We also like to see executive committee members serve as sponsors for specific capabilities that need to be created in the new organization and use the leadership conference to give visibility to these initiatives. It reinforces the importance of capability building, and it draws resources to work streams. When a top operating executive in the business acts as the sponsor for something such as customer relationship management or commercial excellence, it sends a very powerful signal. If each of the major P&L unit heads shepherds one of the new capabilities, they are now working together in *enterprise leadership*.

ESTABLISH THE RIGHT PROJECT INFRASTRUCTURE

A substantial shift of organization design is a major undertaking and requires the kind of infrastructure and leadership that any major program would. In every case, these initiatives are a complex set of work streams—a related group of projects—with myriad teams managing diverse initiatives over a relatively long period of time. The effort needs strong program leadership and the infrastructure that goes with it.

Assigning a heavyweight leader to oversee the entire program is a good place to start. The most progress in the change effort happens when a valuable executive is pulled out of an operating unit and placed in charge of the overall initiative.

A project management organization (PMO) is usually an important part of the program infrastructure. Often, organization transformation includes work streams focused on building shared services organizations, structural cost reductions, and process and systems redesign. These diverse efforts should be tied together under a single PMO, where the various project plans are managed and linkages are made among the work streams, particularly if multiple vendors and consultants are engaged. In addition to project managers, put some process redesign, change management, and organization development staff in the PMO. In this way an interdisciplinary team will look holistically at the work and ensure that support from the PMO goes beyond just managing to the project plan milestones. Run a process that connects all the dimensions. Establish overlapping participation across design teams, and plan a rigorous cadence for reviewing progress in every work stream.

As a boutique organization design firm, we often serve as consultants to separate business unit and function design teams, as well as the enterprise organization design track, while IBM, Accenture, or another large firm is supporting an integrated business services strategy, a cost reduction program, and large-scale business process redesign initiatives. Working with multiple outside resources is very common today, but it's important to organize the task clearly and expect the project leader, assisted by the PMO, to oversee the collective effort to avoid confusion. If the design and activation work is being led by internal HR and organization development staff, as we hope it would be, this same integration and coordination is needed.

If you are going to outsource the PMO work to a consulting firm, make certain it is clear what you are contracting for. Ensure that the service provider understands your business well enough to be effective. While they need to bring a sophisticated approach and tools to the task, also be certain they don't overwhelm the organization with unnecessary process. Don't allow consultants to become the visible advocates for specific solutions, such as integrated business services or delayering. The resistors and doubters soon see through the lack of company sponsorship.

Internal organization development staffers play highly varied roles in this work from company to company. It surprises us from time to time how reluctant some HR and organization development professionals tend to be when it comes to digging into this work. This may be due to lack of resources, given the many other things on their plates, but how many other things could be more important than helping to lead an enterprise initiative to reset the organization model? The ideal is to provide a team of HR and organization development staffers a solid grounding in the organization design and activation concepts so that they feel competent and confident, as a function, to work with business teams and put the material to work.

Communication resources are a critical part of the infrastructure to manage major organization realignment. Some companies have terrific resources internally with the experience to lead this work stream. Others do not, and it is important to resolve early on how this work will get done. The communications professional should be in on the program planning process as soon as practical. Communicators need get close to the work and understand it so that they can bring creative ideas to developing and delivering content. The central challenge for communicators is to keep the growth narrative sharp and consistent across all media and with all audiences. When there are tough stories that must be told regarding downsizing or divesting businesses, it is easy for these negative events to hijack the storyline. This is a mistake. We strongly encourage candor and transparency in communication, but when the bigger story is about growth, don't let the bad news take over.

An organizational change is a campaign. Bring one of your digital marketers who knows how to create customer engagement onto the team. Especially if your vision includes aspirations such as increased speed, flexibility, and collaboration, use your communications methods to model these new attributes. Look for opportunities to celebrate early successes. Don't underinvest in communications, engagement, and feedback.

A significant organization change often requires two to three years to take hold and to earn the payoff of change. Executives don't want to hear this, but most know it is true. We tell them to think of their organization as an information-processing and decision-making machine. They are changing the organization—roles, power, rewards— because they want different decisions and outcomes. However, most high-value decisions are, at best, only made a few times a year. Process redesign work may take a number of years, depending on the availability of capital to invest in automation and reporting systems. It takes a number of business cycles for people in new roles and relationships to practice, learn, and adjust. We can accelerate organization learning, and we can set the people at these new interfaces up for success, but we have to finish the play. Being realistic at the top about the timeframe for change is essential.

WORK THE INTERSECTIONS IN THE NEW ORGANIZATION

As we have argued throughout this book, the most value is created in the intersections of the matrix: the horizontal connections from global to local, from business to function, and from internal to external. It is also true that these connections are where the biggest activation challenges lie. The willingness of senior-most executives to get involved in bringing those connections to life is key. In a legacy culture where senior leaders manage their P&L centers in a silo-oriented fashion, this is even more difficult—a chicken-and-egg kind of problem.

Executive leaders can and should role model the change. This can be a difficult balance between actively coaching leaders in the handshake and avoiding solving all their problems for them. As we argued in the chapter on matrix-ready leaders, the goal is to become a learning organization. The CEO and direct reports should watch for those learning moments to be coaches, and walk the talk on the new operating model.

The CEO should think hard about which top executives go into the key roles in the global operating model. We have worked with CEOs who have been willing to remove senior executives during or even before the design process, when it is clear they are not likely to be effective in the new culture. We have also worked with those who just reshuffled the existing cast and undermined months of design work. Careful consideration should be given to staffing decisions for roles that are pivotal in bringing the new organization to life. An example might be the head of a new global business unit, a role that should be filled by a candidate with a collaborative leadership style and the credibility of having worked in international markets. Another key staffing decision would be the global leader of a major function that is expected to drive an entirely new global agenda and set of capabilities. When Denise Morrison, CEO at Campbell's Soup, started ambitious design work on a global, integrated business services organization, she staffed the position with a very high-potential general manager who had been running a large part of the core business.

MEASURE PROGRESS AND MAKE COURSE CORRECTIONS

The CEO and executive team should role model balanced attention to quarterly results and the organizational health initiatives that will deliver future growth and profitability. The real priorities of the organization become very clear in the business review forums, especially to middle managers who spend hours or days preparing for these sessions. The heads of the business units should be held accountable for the activation of the new organization, and they should hold their middle managers accountable through regular reviews of progress. As part of the business review sessions, draw team members back to the growth imperative and the logic behind the new operating model. If it is not part of the formal agenda, it won't be seen as important. Repetition is a key part of the process.

Use the five activators as the focus of measurement. What changes in each of the five are the critical elements of the new organization model? What level of progress would we expect to see after 90 days, six months, and 12 months? What additional support do the operating teams need to bring to the handshake partnerships, or to shift innovation investments to programs that have growth potential in developing markets? Expect learning to progress through repeated strategy and budgeting cycles. What did we learn from the last strategic planning cycle, and how can joint global and local strategies be more robust the next time around? Table 9.1 provides an activation checklist.

Collaboration can and should be measured, also. Look for positive examples of global and local players working together to bring an existing product into a new market, and celebrate those wins very publicly. Senior leaders should encourage teams to go visit other parts of the company to find out what's working. Lift and shift the internal bright spots as far and wide as possible. Get peer feedback for participants across the handshake: Am I easy to work with? Are my team and I responsive? Support new leaders in big new roles, but don't let

Table 9.1 A summary of critical practices to consider during the activation and design process.

Activation To-Do's

* Use the design process road map—and take an activation mindset from the beginning through the end of the design process.

* Create a project plan to manage the entire change program, with specific calendar action items for each of the five activators.

* Build leadership alignment into the plan, starting with the executive team. Get the cards on the table, and watch out for passive resistors.

* Use large-group design sessions to build a broad base of support.

* Assign executive committee members to act as sponsors for building new capabilities and other critical enterprise changes.

* Put the right project infrastructure in place to manage the overall program, including a strong project leader.

* Dedicate communications resources to the change process, and utilize all available media to reach people.

* Focus management energy on the intersections in the matrix, the horizontal connections between global and local or business and function.

* Measure progress continually and make course corrections along the way.

* Be prepared to stay the course (for up to two years or more on major transformations).

those who refuse to behave consistently with the new model carry on for too long.

Adjustments to the organization design and to the five activators are common in deploying new organization models. Some functions are overresourced initially, and others are underresourced. A council of worldwide marketers may seem like a great idea during the design phase but may turn out to be a waste of time, or it may not have the right remit and have to be rechartered. The strategic and annual operating planning cycle may not have the integrating effects that were expected with the global–local handshakes. These corrections should not be delayed unnecessarily, but they also should not be hurried. Take the time to assess why the change has not delivered the desired effects before rushing to change it.

After 12 and again after 24 months, more formal methods for assessing progress will be useful. Chapter 7, "The Organizational Health-Check Toolkit," includes a number of assessment and survey instruments that are useful for this purpose. If surveys or interview questions with rating scales are used at the beginning of the design process to assess needs and establish a baseline, bring the same questions back and measure the progress against baseline data.

Summary of the Chapter

- The design and activation of a global operating model typically takes two years or more of engaged, disciplined program management.

- Activation needs to be considered throughout the design process and well beyond initial implementation.

- Gaining alignment across the top executive team, throughout the design and activation process, is a critical step to assure that passive-aggressive and other change-resistant behaviors are avoided.

- The most effective CEO behaviors include expressing a clear, strong case for change while welcoming debate and diverse viewpoints, followed by firm closure and behavioral expectations for the executive team.

- Design and activation workshops with a large cross section of the leadership are powerful change-management events that produce learning while building ownership and buy-in to the new organization model and culture.

- Some of the most important activation work will be focused on the intersections between global and local businesses and functions in implementing role clarity, aligned business planning processes, and decision rights.

- Staffing key orchestrating roles in the global matrix will be one of the most important decisions in the entire activation process.

- Progress should be measured, and leadership should anticipate the need for course corrections during the activation process.

CHAPTER 10

When the Activators Work Together

ACROSS THE FIVE ACTIVATORS

The bridge to performance is built by developing the activators as parts of an integrated management system. The real power of the five activators model is in the interdependence and mutual reinforcement across the five. No matter how motivated and skilled a set of managers is, if the organization hasn't provided the forums and processes to connect and have the right conversations, a lot of well-intentioned individual effort will be wasted. Conversely, no amount of reengineering of management processes will make up for a management team unwilling or unable to engage in collaborative behavior.

The activators also work together at a more subtle level. For example, identification of the anchor layer sets up who needs to come together in the business unit/region handshake. Well-designed target setting and performance review meetings over time build trust and social capital. Functions that are designed explicitly as integrative mechanisms help to move talent around the globe, creating a pipeline of ready leaders able to engage in innovation and execution networks.

In simple parlance, there are three key outcomes that are expected in a well-activated, global operating model:

1. *The right connections* are made across businesses and functions that create value together.

2. *The right conversations* take place to align objectives, to make effective operating decisions, and to manage the ongoing performance of the business.

3. *The right know-how* is built through active talent development practices that deliver a bench of matrix-ready leaders.

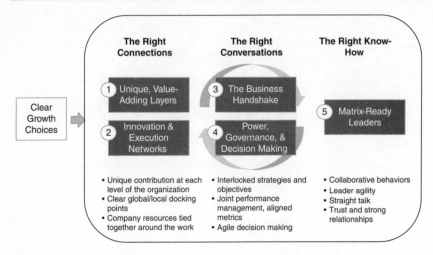

Figure 10.1   The five activators for the global operating model.

Let's review the activators, with emphasis on the interaction among the five. (See Figure 10.1.)

THE RIGHT CONNECTIONS

Structure is still a critical element of organization design. The task is to define the working connections among global business units and regional or local business units, as well as connections among worldwide functions and the businesses they support. Two of the five activators help to assure the right connections are built into the organization.

Activator #1: Unique Value-Adding Layers

The fewest possible layers, each with a unique value-adding contribution, will reduce complexity and will enable delegation and faster decision making. Collaboration across the hierarchy is key. It is especially important to enable clear, direct partnerships between global and regional units. Infrastructure and support activities should be consolidated where practical and not replicated at multiples levels.

Interaction with Other Activators

- The anchor layer enables a clear docking station for the handshake between global and local roles.

- Innovation networks can be organized among global and local or regional centers that are working at the same level of organization.

- Execution networks and communities of practice can be established among functional teams that are working in the field units.

- Eliminating overlapping layers of responsibilities provides greater development opportunities for high-potential leaders. Anchor-level business management roles are the training ground for the company's next generation of top executives.

Activator #2: Innovation and Execution Networks

Today, companies are setting up formal networks of global and local capability with guidance from the center as an alternative to centralization, in order to gain the benefits of both agility and leverage. Ideas can move not just from the center to the operating units, but also across business units and geographies to generate innovation. Marketers in global brand, category, or product teams can be networked to country- or region-based commercial marketers, who work together to create marketing programs and new product-innovation ideas that can be leveraged across international markets.

Execution networks can drive digital capabilities and shared services across multiple markets, retaining local flexibility while leveraging expensive resources and assuring a single architecture.

Interaction with Other Activators

- Center-based leadership roles should be staffed with agile leaders who are eager to seek out ideas from field-based units and able to sell ideas across the globe through strong influence skills.

- A handful of decision rights focused on go/no go, funding, and standardization decisions will be useful to help make networks fully functional.

- Budget ownership may be centralized or distributed out in the units (or there may be a combination of both), but access to resources is critical to executing ideas managed by networks.

- Matrix-ready leaders understand the value of building internal and external communities of players with shared interests around a brand, a market, or an internal shared service.

THE RIGHT CONVERSATIONS

Organization design should enable the right conversations—patterns of thought and behavior—aligned against the short- and long-term goals of a business. Agile response to international business environments requires real-time problem solving among people who remain focused on the right outcomes.

We have explored two critical activators that help shape the right conversations through smart operating mechanisms, including annual operating plans, goal alignment, budgeting, and performance management practices.

Activator #3: The Business Handshake

Once the anchor operating units are identified in the structure, a disciplined effort should be made to formalize the most important partnerships in the nodes in the matrix that generate the most value. The handshake is the agreement across organizational boundaries on what results will be delivered and how. An integrated planning process connects strategic plans with operating targets and budgeting, and in the handshake, it connects the partners across business lines, geographies, and functions.

After interlocking targets and resource plans are set, the principals in the handshake adhere to a performance-management cadence to manage results at the right level of detail, with the right data, and with the right frequency.

Interaction with Other Activators

- The global/local handshake is facilitated by a vertical organizational structure made up of clear and complementary roles.

- Power and decision making are shared by partners in the handshake. Decision rights are aligned with the specific accountabilities that each partner owns.

- Matrix-ready leaders are critical to making the handshakes effective. Willingness to delegate, and willingness to trust peers to act on behalf of the partnership are critical to speed.

Activator #4: Power, Governance, and Decision Making

Decision making takes place in the context of company and national cultures. In a global operating model, organizational culture must support the right balance of global, local, and functional influence, and value empowerment of cross-boundary teams. Companies can design better, faster management forums for making enterprise and operating unit decisions. The roles of executive committees, operating committees, portfolio management process, and strategic councils should be focused and linked together to provide clear direction for business units.

Decision rights among global and local roles (and among business units and enterprise functions) are focused on the highest-value decisions in the handshake. Partners in the handshake work together with a regular cadence, transparency, and action focus. When effective decisions can be made swiftly by one leader or one business unit, unnecessary collaboration should be eliminated—and meetings taken off people's calendars.

But tension in the matrix is natural and exists for the benefit of shareholders and customers. Healthy conflict draws energy to sources of value, and competing voices work together to serve the short- and long-term interests of the company, however challenging it may seem on a given issue.

Interaction with Other Activators

- Governance forums are easier to configure when unnecessary layers have been eliminated. People can be invited into these forums based on contribution rather than title or status in the hierarchy.

- Integrator roles (such as sales and operations planning roles) can be placed in the center of execution networks to facilitate complex interactions. Decision rights often fall naturally to these integrator roles due to their ability to see the entire flow of work from end to end.

- Matrix-ready leaders are willing to delegate, and they are willing and able to be decisive while remaining sensitive to the impact their actions have on partners in the matrix.

THE RIGHT KNOW-HOW

In companies that fully activate the global operating model, a pipeline of matrix-ready leadership is the result of disciplined assessment, selection and development practices, clearly defined behavioral criteria, and deep commitment to talent development throughout the company.

Activator #5: Matrix-Ready Leaders

Leaders who succeed in the global matrix can and should be selected and developed for learning agility, influence skills, and ability to engage in the tensions among naturally competing priorities. These personal traits and skills, learned through the right experiences, bring the other activators to life. Building a global talent pipeline is a core capability for companies that want to activate a global operating model.

A great deal of research has been done to define characteristics of effective global leaders. Businesses would do well to adopt the core insights of this large body of work and concentrate on assembling practical talent-management applications for putting these well-defined behavioral criteria to work, rather than inventing their own competency models. Talent development is a culture trait that has been a source of competitive advantage for many global companies.

Interaction with Other Activators

- Companies that create positive environments with fewer hierarchical layers, effective networks, and simple decision rights are more likely to retain high-potential leaders who are motivated to make a difference.

- Degrees of uncertainty are natural in a large, matrix organization, and matrix-ready leaders are comfortable with some ambiguity, are effective at managing conflict, and are willing to share power.

- Network assignments that are big on accountability but provide low formal authority are powerful development assignments for high-potential leaders.

- The best global leadership development systems develop people and the organization simultaneously. Building effective networks teaches nuanced leadership skills to the participants.

■ ■ ■

Activation is an ongoing process, shaped by external events and fueled by reflection and learning. We believe that a leadership team that invests in activation will avoid some of the need for the periodic large-scale restructurings that can be so disruptive to business flows and employee productivity. With activation, you are always organizing and evolving, rather than chasing false stability and then having to reorganize.

We have observed an attitude and a cultural quality to companies that seem to make the most progress with the journey. Here are some of the traits and thought processes we have found compelling in the companies we have worked with:

- Global business is a puzzle, and we must work to solve it in every market we choose to serve.

- Wisdom is found in all parts of the world; let's organize to take advantage of that fact.

- We are going to make mistakes; let's learn from them.

- Complexity is inevitable, but we should not let our own internal processes and structures make it any worse than it needs to be.

- We are designing new ways of working, changing the management system; let's keep our eye on the big picture.

Companies that compete globally must balance the need for both global and local perspectives in decision making, but the complexity of managing global operating models is a difficult challenge in the search for new sources of growth.

Activation is the deliberate and adaptive creation of new work, decisions, and business outcomes gained through the repetition and refinement of management processes and interactions over time. Leaders who embrace activation will find that they have created the blueprint for building the bridge from organization design to business performance.

CHAPTER 11

The Organization
Health-Check Tool Kit

T wo years into the implementation of its new global operating model, a large capital equipment company contacted us to discuss some challenges they were facing in getting their matrix organization to be effective. Five global product platforms were expected to interact directly with four regional customer organizations, supported by global technical and marketing functions. In the initial phone conversation, two executives described a recent top-200 leadership conference the CEO held, focused on an ambitious five-year growth strategy. In break-out sessions during the conference (and subsequent debriefs in plenary session), the agenda topics were overshadowed by concerns that managers were expressing about disconnects and overlaps in the roles of the global product groups and the regional commercial business units. Many of the operating managers were also expressing a number of concerns about overreach by corporate functions that were driving more costs than value into the businesses.

This is not an unusual account of events in the period following a major restructuring of a company. Concerns bubble up out of the operations in a number of ways. The trick is to separate the noise—discomfort or resistance to new ways of working—from genuine effectiveness problems that need attention. Our colleagues in the industrial products company had wisely decided to conduct a set of interviews with a cross section of the extended leadership team, a process they referred to as an organizational health check. The interviews were conducted by a well-regarded consulting group who provided a granular and insightful report on the findings. The interviews revealed substantial support for the two-year-old organizational model, but highlighted many concerns about its implementation. The data were anchored in metrics including customer focus, decision-making speed, and collaboration. A project charter was prepared, aimed at refining the global organization design. The parameters were clear. The organization structure would remain intact with minor adjustments; the primary focus of improvement efforts would be on operating mechanisms, role clarity, and leadership skills and behaviors.

Bringing a global operating model to life requires sophisticated and coordinated ways of thinking and behaving across the management ranks. Company leadership should not expect to get it all right at the initial rollout. Better to design with the expectation that as people work through real situations, there will be learning and adjustments. We suggest building in an organizational health check at the 12- and 24-month marks after the majority of implementation is complete. The purpose of the health check is to identify what is working well and what needs to be fine-tuned or added. Fully implementing one of these organizations is a multiyear journey that requires sustained energy from leadership.

The organization health check is not limited to an after-action review of a major organizational realignment. It can be used whenever there is a strategic redirection. We believe the CEOs of every mid- to large-cap company should make their organization's fitness for growth central to their strategic dialogue and know how to start the conversation.

In the summer of 2014, Nike CEO Mark Parker challenged his senior team to determine whether their organization's architecture could support doubling revenues over an ambitious planning horizon. Parker and his team are faced with enormous pressure to continue delivering the outsized returns that shareholders have come to expect from Nike. In our experience, Parker was exceptionally forward thinking in asking his team the central design question of an aggressive growth strategy—*Are we fit for future growth?* Most executive leadership teams do not proactively design their organizations for growth. Instead, they often plan growth strategies for the future and then make organizational changes in response to performance gaps seen in the rearview mirror.

What follows is a set of tools for assessing how well the organization is able to support the strategic intentions and then activating the organization where there are misalignments. The first section of the tool kit includes a survey and an interview guide for completing an overall scan of the effectiveness of activation across the five activators. The subsequent sections include more specific assessment and intervention tools specific to each of the five activators. These are all examples from our own practice. Rather than make them generic and lose the robustness that comes with specificity, we have left in some questions or elements that relate to a particular context. Of course, you should customize all of these to your context.

SUMMARY HEALTH CHECK DIAGNOSTICS

Tool #1: Five Activators: Survey

Application: Survey a cross section of leaders as part of a broader assessment of activation effectiveness. Consider combining data with qualitative interviews with a subset of respondents. Prioritize areas for action.

	Not at All True	Some-what True	Very True
	1 2	3	4 5
Unique Value-Adding Layers			
1. We are vigilant about removing unnecessary layers, P&L units, and divisions that duplicate decision making. We avoid overlapping roles in our organizational levels.			
2. It is clear to global product or brand teams who their business partners are out in the regions. We have defined clear points for collaboration in the matrix.			

(continued)

	Not at All True	Some- what True		Very True
	1	2	3	4	5

3. Trade-off decisions are made at the right level in our business unit structure. We avoid suboptimal decisions made at too high or too low a level in the organization.

4. We do not have unnecessary layers of functional work and resources (e.g., HR, finance, marketing, IT, etc.) up and down in the organization. Each level plays a clear, unique, value-adding role.

5. The cost structure of our overall organization is sustainable. We have minimal structural waste.

Innovation and Execution Networks

6. Our global and local teams work well together to come up with the best growth initiatives for the company. They collaborate well around a common agenda without worrying about who is in charge.

(continued)

	Not at All True	Some- what True	Very True
	1 2	3 4	5

7. New product and other growth initiatives can come from anywhere in the organization, and we have a process to scale them and lift and shift ideas to other parts of the company.

8. We are able to capture operational synergies that create value for our customers across our operating divisions and/or business units.

9. We are able to move our best growth ideas and initiatives across geographies, brands, and divisions.

The Business Handshake

10. Our strategic and operational planning process results in priorities that focus management attention on clear growth choices.

(continued)

	Not at All True		Some-what True		Very True
	1	2	3	4	5

11. Growth and performance targets are clearly aligned vertically and horizontally in the matrix. Global and local players work together with interlocked business plans.

12. We are agile as a company at shifting resources and investments to growth hot spots.

13. Our metrics and business performance reviews put the right data in front of the right people to bring the root causes of issues to the surface and enable action. We enable candid and productive conversations.

14. Business results are co-owned by empowered, global-local partners in the matrix.

Decision Making

15. Our executive committee members invest the right amount of time in enterprise leadership, not just delivering against their individual business plans.

(continued)

	Not at All True		Some-what True		Very True
	1	2	3	4	5

16. We have effective governance forums for making decisions about company-wide investment priorities and key capabilities (e.g., customer experience, innovation, brand building, quality, etc.)

17. We have defined decision-making principles and called out clear decision rights where needed for product, market, and functional leaders in the matrix.

18. We delegate real responsibility down to the right levels of the business, through formal mechanisms as well as cultural and behavioral norms.

19. We are effective at balancing the competing pressures of short versus long term, profit versus growth, and whole-company versus division results.

(continued)

	Not at All True	Some- what True	Very True
	1 2	3	4 5

Matrix-Ready Leaders

20. We have invested time and resources to help leaders navigate the matrix through education, skill building, network building, and coaching. Our leaders understand the role our organizational design plays in creating more value for shareholders and customers.

21. We invest management time and energy in building relationships and trust among leaders across the organization. We are good at straight talk and candor.

22. We utilize the right competencies for selecting and developing global leaders (who demonstrate learning agility, ability to manage complex trade-offs, trust building, influencing across boundaries, global mindset, organization architecting, and community building).

(continued)

	Not at All True		Some-what True		Very True
	1	2	3	4	5

23. We utilize robust practices for building a global pipeline of leadership talent through shared talent review forums, rotations and mobility, and deliberate use of developmental experiences.

24. We have a strong bench of ready-now leaders who can be effective in global leadership roles in the company.

Tool #2: Organizational Health Check: Interview Guide

Application: Conduct interviews with a cross section of middle and senior leadership to evaluate effectiveness of the activation work on the global operating model, 12–24 months after implementation.

1. Describe your area of responsibility and your organization.

2. Tell me about your key partners in the matrix.

3. What do you need from each of your key three to four partners in order to be effective in your role?

4. Which of those expectations are fully met and which are not today?

(continued)

5. How would you characterize the overall effectiveness of the matrix (from your vantage point) when it comes to delivering results for the business overall? Are there misses in results stemming from our matrixed organization? Example, please.

6. How would you describe the clarity of your own role and the roles of your key partners in the matrix? Explain.

    Not Effective   1   2   3   4   5   Highly Effective

7. How would you evaluate the degree of alignment among your objectives and those of your partners?

    Not Effective   1   2   3   4   5   Highly Effective

8. How decisive and timely do you believe we are as an organization? Explain.

    Not Effective   1   2   3   4   5   Highly Effective

9. What kinds of decisions tend to produce the most tension? How clear are the decision rights for these areas? In general, how much alignment/agreement is there on who has decision rights for particular areas?

10. How candid with each other are people in the organization when tough conversations need to take place? Examples, please. What gets in the way?

    Not Effective   1   2   3   4   5   Highly Effective

11. How would you describe the quality of your relationship with your key partners? Why?

    Not Effective   1   2   3   4   5   Highly Effective

12. How would you describe the quality of your relationship with colleagues within your organization?

    Not Effective   1   2   3   4   5   Highly Effective

    (continued)

13. What role do incentives and reward systems play in fostering or hindering collaboration?

14. What are we not talking about that we should be? Why and how important is that to our business?

Unique Value-Adding Layers

Tool #3: Unique Value-Adding Layers, Organizational Structure Effectiveness: Interview Guide

Application: Interview a cross section of global and regional business and/or functional leaders who must work together in a matrix relationship to determine how effective the structure is.

1. Tell me about your organization and role.

2. What are the primary strategic priorities for your business (or the company as a whole) now?

3. Given those priorities, what is working well with the current organization? How has organization helped drive the growth results you have seen?

4. What is not working well today in that regard?

5. Tell me about the interdependencies between this business and the others. Who are your key partners? What are the key points of integration?

6. How effective are the connection points between your team and your partner(s)?

7. How clear are the accountabilities for the profit and loss (P&L) in this business?

8. Who is accountable for managing each product offering today in this business from a life cycle and P&L point of view? (Probe scope of roles and links to marketing.)

(continued)

9. To what extent does each layer in the organization have a unique value-adding role to play? How would you describe those roles?

10. Where do you see potential opportunities to simplify the structure and reduce waste or duplication of effort?

11. Are there changes in structure that could make collaboration more effective?

12. What common processes will need to be developed or harmonized to make a new structure effective?

13. What do you see as the most important challenges in implementing a new organization design?

Tool #4: Horizontal Role Definition by Process (Brand Company Example)

Application: One of several templates that can be used to define roles at a high level, by process. It may be effective to use this draft as a starting point in working with a cross-region, cross-business team.

Key Processes	Global Business Unit	Regional Market Organization	Local Market Organization
Brand strategy	Manage brands, product mix, positioning	Execute brand strategy	Execute brand strategy
Brand image	Define brand image	—	—
Consumer knowledge	Synthesize regional insight and ideas	Provide support, consumer data, and insights for tailoring	Provide support, consumer data, and insights for tailoring
New product portfolio management	Develop plan based on growth strategies	Provide input to global plan; develop regional market plans	Provide input to global and regional plans
New product development	Develop new products	Provide regional sales forecast	Prioritize launches based on incremental sales and contribution

(*continued*)

New product launch	Set launch target priorities	Align target priorities for region	Align target priorities for country
Sales and distribution	Negotiate global distribution partnership	Deliver regional sales and distribution	Deliver local sales and distribution
Advertising and promotion	Design advertising campaigns	Execute ad campaigns	Execute ad campaigns
Accountability	Global P&L contribution	Revenue, market share, cost of selling, channel health	Revenue, market share, cost of selling, channel health

Innovation and Execution Networks

Tool #5: Trust and Candor: Survey

Application: Survey a cross section of leaders working in a matrix organization to measure levels of trust and candor in the working relationships. May combine with interview data as part of an organizational health check.

Indicate to what extent you believe the company experiences these effects as a result of lack of trust and candor in our culture:

1. It is somewhat common to see passive-aggressive behavior: say one thing in the room and another outside the room (or hallway conversations expressing negative attitudes to a decision).

    Not At All True   1   2   3   4   5   Very True

2. We do not escalate important issues that should be escalated to top management; better to stay quiet.

    Not At All True   1   2   3   4   5   Very True

(continued)

3. We lack vigorous debate on priorities or issues when they involve "sacred cows."

    Not At All True   1   2   3   4   5   Very True

4. Leaders don't speak up in leadership meetings about things outside their immediate bailiwick (so we don't leverage all our expertise).

    Not At All True   1   2   3   4   5   Very True

5. Some business units may avoid working or engaging with functional groups especially if there are sensitive issues (possibly not leveraging our technology).

    Not At All True   1   2   3   4   5   Very True

6. We are not willing to say "no" to things or eliminate work, so we keep adding more work (and/or resources).

    Not At All True   1   2   3   4   5   Very True

7. We may not be completely candid about performance issues in the business (or with individuals). We are a "good news" culture.

    Not At All True   1   2   3   4   5   Very True

8. We may be reluctant to set stretch targets (and then budgets become a negotiation).

    Not At All True   1   2   3   4   5   Very True

9. What other ways have you seen a potential lack of trust / candor play out?

Potential causes of a lack of trust and candor in our culture.

Indicate to what extent you believe each of the following is true:

1. Setting stretch goals just puts you in a situation where you are more likely to fail. We don't take into account the difficulty in some of the goals we set.

    Not At All True   1   2   3   4   5   Very True

2. When we have debated priorities there have been projects and initiatives that just stay on the list because of their history or sponsorship; it's pointless to debate them.

    Not At All True   1   2   3   4   5   Very True

3. Collaboration has become a somewhat politically correct concept, and people are afraid to appear that they are not collaborative. Better to just stay quiet.

    Not At All True   1   2   3   4   5   Very True

4. There is a perception that some of the players (in the businesses and the functions) may be in it for their careers more than business results.

    Not At All True   1   2   3   4   5   Very True

5. Business units may perceive some functions often make their initiatives or support proposals too complex or too expensive and just haven't shown enough value. Easier to do it ourselves.

    Not At All True   1   2   3   4   5   Very True

(continued)

6. We just aren't investing as much time and energy in relationships, especially outside the home office, due to all the things on our plates.

   Not At All True   1   2   3   4   5   Very True

7. Some of our trust issues are caused by a perception that some of the players are not fully competent at what they do.

   Not At All True   1   2   3   4   5   Very True

8. Some functional groups have shared business unit compliance or other sensitive information ("dirty laundry") with senior leaders before showing it to the business unit.

   Not At All True   1   2   3   4   5   Very True

9. We work too much inside our silos to create a "one team" attitude.

   Not At All True   1   2   3   4   5   Very True

10. Senior executives will sometimes ask for input on issues where they have already made up their minds.

    Not At All True   1   2   3   4   5   Very True

11. Sometimes when people are candid, they don't seem to be heard or feel brushed off. Not enough examples where candor leads to a real change of course.

    Not At All True   1   2   3   4   5   Very True

12. We may distrust some colleagues because we don't want to lose control over our area of responsibility.

    Not At All True   1   2   3   4   5   Very True

13. What other ways have you seen a potential lack of trust/candor play out?

List 3–5 tension areas where decision rights are not clear between business units and functions. Focus on examples that are important points of confusion and slow decision making. Try to be specific. Examples might include:

a. Ongoing operational decisions

b. Global staffing decisions

c. Pace and number of standards to be implemented in a business

d. Specific compliance areas

Tool #6: Network and Relationships Map

Application: Use at all levels when people move into new roles and need to proactively build new and positive working relationships across organizational boundaries. Can also be used to understand patterns of existing networks across business units. (See Figure 11.1.)

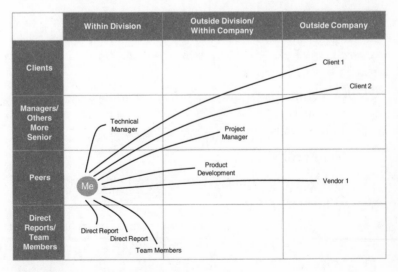

Figure 11.1   Relationship map.

(continued)

A. Write the names of 10–12 people that will be critical to your effectiveness in the matrix. They may be people you should have or do have a relationship with. Note what type of network each falls into.

B. Transfer the names and roles you identified in the previous step to the appropriate section of the relationship map.

- Clients

- Managers

- Peers

- Direct reports or team members (those you manage directly or indirectly)

C. Draw a line from the center circle ("me") to each name.

Tool #7: Contracting

Application: Use with network team members to contract alignment of mutual support needs across the matrix. This is an easy and high-impact activity as part of the team launch or a management conference.

Choose someone in the room from your relationship map whom you need to work with to achieve your objectives. Try to pick someone you don't see face-to-face all the time.

Plan and then hold this conversation with the person.

1. "My most important objectives for the coming six months are...."

2. "This is what I need from you to help me achieve my objectives...."

3. "You should know the following about my work style in order work most effectively with me...."

Identify goals and priorities that you believe you share with this partner and identify which ones are aligned, which are

(continued)

different, and which are potentially conflicting. Then identify actions to reach alignment.

Goals and Priorities	Actions
Aligned: Where are we aligned—i.e., we have the same or similar overall goal?	How can we use this to create forward momentum?
Different: Where are our goals, needs, and agendas simply different but not necessarily affecting others in a critical way?	What needs to happen to prevent this from becoming a problem in the future?
Conflicting: Where are we in a true polarity dilemma?	What steps do we need to take urgently to resolve this conflict ourselves... or with the support of others?

THE BUSINESS HANDSHAKE

Tool #8: Business-Market Team Effectiveness

Application: Survey all the members of a business unit-market (or business unit-function) handshake team as part of the team launch or several months after the team has been working together. Facilitate a discussion of the results with the team to prioritize improvement areas.

Decision Making

1. Decisions are pushed down to lowest practical level and to managers who are best positioned to make effective decisions.

   Agree   1   2   3   4   5   Disagree

   (continued)

2. The handshake is the primary way of setting agreements on plans between global and regional players.

    Agree   1   2   3   4   5   Disagree

3. The "51 percent vote" is clear on all items, including who owns this golden vote on critical issues.

    Agree   1   2   3   4   5   Disagree

4. We do not overuse the golden vote. Most of the time we are able to get to agreement on key decisions between global and regional.

    Agree   1   2   3   4   5   Disagree

5. Our executives are effective at letting us run our business for the most part, without unnecessary interference.

    Agree   1   2   3   4   5   Disagree

6. When decisions are made between global and regional, they are not revisited; we get on with taking action in a timely manner.

    Agree   1   2   3   4   5   Disagree

Goals and Metrics

1. Our goals and ambitions for the handshake are clear and documented in our plans.

    Agree   1   2   3   4   5   Disagree

2. The planning process for strategic and annual targets is effective.

    Agree   1   2   3   4   5   Disagree

(continued)

3. We work well together to align objectives. There are no obvious disconnects in the global and regional plans.

   Agree   1   2   3   4   5   Disagree

4. We have a set of effective KPIs in place to track the progress of our business-market handshake.

   Agree   1   2   3   4   5   Disagree

Roles

1. The roles of individuals in the handshake are clear. They do not overlap and there are no gaps.

   Agree   1   2   3   4   5   Disagree

2. We have clear points of connection between the global and the regional roles. We are clear on how to work together at the interface of roles.

   Agree   1   2   3   4   5   Disagree

Process and Meeting Rhythms

1. The right people participate in our meetings at the right times. Our meetings and routines are a priority for people.

   Agree   1   2   3   4   5   Disagree

2. We follow a well-established cadence for reviewing results and solving problems.

   Agree   1   2   3   4   5   Disagree

3. Our progress is reviewed only once a month with all the right participants attending.

   Agree   1   2   3   4   5   Disagree

(continued)

4. We focus on the right topics in our meetings, including looking ahead to what should have our attention in the future.

    Agree   1   2   3   4   5   Disagree

5. We focus on business dialogue rather than just the financials.

    Agree   1   2   3   4   5   Disagree

6. The frequency of our meetings is about right.

    Agree   1   2   3   4   5   Disagree

Relationships, Candor, and Trust

1. We communicate effectively with each other and on a regular basis.

    Agree   1   2   3   4   5   Disagree

2. Conflicts are brought up among team members, and we manage the tensions for the benefit of the business.

    Agree   1   2   3   4   5   Disagree

3. People are candid on this team; they speak their minds.

    Agree   1   2   3   4   5   Disagree

4. We trust each other to do the right thing for the business.

    Agree   1   2   3   4   5   Disagree

Tool #9: Horizontal Linkages Discussion (Health Care Company Example)

Application: Use the template to help groups work through key horizontal linkages between two or more business units and/or functions. Use the content to identify process needs or other integrating methods for assuring effective linkages.

(continued)

Key Partners	Key Linkage Areas	To Accomplish
Central commercial marketing, clinical franchises, value creation marketing, operations	Strategic planning (clinical franchise)	• Effective launch • Effective input to long-range plan • Effective P&L management • Service-level requirements • Reporting enhancements • Content management and syndication • Program execution
Central commercial marketing, clinical franchises and value creation marketing, operations (and functional partners)	Market development strategy	• A strategy to grow the market widely owned by commercial management and interlocked with ops and clinical franchises • Reach new customers • Prioritize sales targets in a footprint • Plan to drive share in submarkets and customer segments • Align resources against priorities (including clinical franchises) • Interlocked expectations with operations and clinical franchises • Definitive tactical plans for submarkets including investment

(continued)

Key Partners	Key Linkage Areas	To Accomplish
Clinical franchises, regional vice president of commercial, and regional vice president of operations	Annual business plan and business review cadence	• One-year view of the market strategy • Interlocked plan of record with Clinical Franchises and operation • Linkage with annual budget • Alignment on resource priorities (interlocked) • Clearly aligned metrics
Clinical franchises, sales directors, RVPs, commercial marketing	Balanced score card process plus incentives	• Getting to the right sales mix

POWER, GOVERNANCE, AND DECISION MAKING

Tool #10: Mapping Governance Forums and Key Processes (Consumer Products Company Example)

Application: Can be used to map out the roles and responsibilities of key decision-making groups, relative to core management processes to assure clear intersections.

(continued)

	Annual Strategic & Operations Planning	Regional Customer Management	Innovation Portfolio Management	New Product Development	Global and Regional Brand Management	Global and Regional Mergers and Acquisitions
Executive committee	Set strategic and financial parameters				Review proposed plans	Approve proposals
Operating committee			Articulate needs, align category plans	Manage assigned projects		
Corporate functions	Function strategies					
Regional executive teams	Strategic growth plan, annual targets	Key customer plans	Strategic business plan	Align resources in the Annual Operating Plan (AOP)	Align resources in AOP	Sourcing
Global category teams	Strategic growth plan		Innovation strategies			
Global process owners	Oversee process			Oversee process		Oversee process

(continued)

Tool #11: Decision Rights Grid (Consumer Products Company Example)

Application: Global business unit and regional business unit work together to identify decision rights, focused on key areas of tension. When agreement can't be reached through collaboration, the 51 percent golden vote is identified.

Collaborative Decision Areas	Definition	Decides
Product portfolio strategy	Create an enterprise view of portfolio innovations to support trade-off decisions Metrics to evaluate innovations; recommendations on areas for innovation "Go/no-go" decision to fund innovation; "go/no-go" decision to launch Guidelines on innovation launch process and possible local variances Metrics to evaluate launch success	Global category (51 percent) and regions (49 percent)
Horizontal product lift and shift	Expand existing offerings in new markets: • Identify lift and shift opportunities in portfolios; segmentation of opportunities	Global category (49 percent) and regions (51 percent)

(continued)

Collaborative Decision Areas	Definition	Decides
	• "Go/no-go" decision	
	• Recommendations on brand expansions that are globally consistent versus can vary after shift	
	• Metrics to evaluate lift & shift success	
Annual revenue and contribution target setting	Segment opportunities for organic growth into new spaces Feasibility and fit with strategic vision and goals; segmentation of proposed new business models Testing, timeline, and geographic rollout for selected business models Recommended changes and investments "Go/no-go" decision Metrics to evaluate launch success	Global category (51 percent) and regions (49 percent)
Strategic pricing	Set the pricing corridors on a worldwide basis, for adaptation by commercial regions for competitive pricing levels.	Global category (51 percent) and regions (49 percent)
Advertising and promotion spending	In-region media plans and agency contracts for annual plan, guided by handshake strategy and AOP for the region.	Global category (49 percent) and regions (51 percent)

(continued)

Tool #12: Decision Scenario (Deep-Water Drilling Example with Oil and Gas Exploration Company)

Application: Work with cross-boundary units to clarify the decision-making process in critical tension areas that involve complex issues with very high financial and technical consequences.

Issue	Drilling contract requirements exceed current contractual arrangement. How to manage a potential expanded drilling program versus paying for an idle rig?
Partners	Wells group, exploration management, business unit management, other international, supply chain management. Angola external partners.
Tension Areas	Trust in decision quality. Past experience by some stakeholders is that decisions are not transparent. Risk/benefit analysis may not be credible or rigorous.
Conversations	Joint review of governance to confirm which group will coordinate the assembly of options for managing currently available rig days. How will we align objectives—early in the process, including management bonus targets? Agree if decision will be periodically revisited or not with new data.
Decision Enablers	Generation of clear options. Agreement on decision points. Decision criteria. No compartmentalized information. More input on economics. Ability to valuate opportunities objectively. Willingness to portray risks accurately with no bias. Willingness to partner quickly up front.

(continued)

Decision Rights	Exploration department has 51 percent tipping vote, but only after extensive engagement with all other partners.
Key Behaviors	Demonstrate enterprise interest in the outcome and trust your colleagues are doing the same. Be candid when you suspect otherwise—and speak with facts. Listen!

MATRIX-READY LEADERS

Tool #13: Global General Manager Talent Review: Facilitator Guide (Consumer Packaged Goods Company Example)

Application: Sample of robust, dialogue-oriented executive committee review of current and future general management talent across major operating regions. Emphasis on candid and active participation in calibration and identifying future moves for key players. One-day session.

Agenda for a Regional Review

Topic	Outcomes	Process	Time
Overview and state of global talent depth	Update on issues, themes, action taken, and overall levels of effectiveness of current situation.	Group presidents (GPs) speak from hard copies of prepared binders (all participants have copies).	25 mins.
Key talent summary, diversity, gaps, and priorities	Draw attention to most critical general management (GM) talent for purposes of visibility and shared ownership for key talent.	GPs speak from overview and analysis template; questions for clarity and potential issues captured on nine-box grid and depth chart (wall charts).	20 mins.

(continued)

Topic	Outcomes	Process	Time
Talent pool readiness grid	Provide current thinking on readiness for key GM jobs, increase visibility, and summarize key gaps/themes; identify questions for debate later.	GPs speak from single-page grid and answer questions for clarity; summarize readiness themes, gaps, and issues; EC peers post pink flags on wall chart names for later debate in cross-region calibration discussion; capture key gaps on walls.	35 mins.
Division president sort on nine-box grid	Provide best thinking on potential/ performance of current division presidents as input to later calibration discussion.	All executive committee (EC) members move to wall charts; GP places sticky names on 9-box and depth charts as starting point for later discussion; peers can place pink flags on question names.	15 mins.
Anticipated regional GM openings	Forecast opportunities and potential moves—list cross-region action items.	Build a flip chart of projected openings as we go for slating at the end of day 2.	15 mins.

Agenda for Cross-Region GM Calibration

Topic	Outcomes	Process	Time
GM 9-box grid division president calibration	Consensus on the placement of all division presidents (DP) in a single 9-box grid; clear picture of potential and summary set of development/ retention action items for top 4–6 players.	With wall charts, overall set of names on Post-its is considered, starting with pink-flagged players; discussion/debate leads to consensus on overall picture.	60 mins.

(continued)

Topic	Outcomes	Process	Time
GM talent pool readiness review	Consensus on placement of all key GM talent against target jobs in terms of readiness; highlight key action items for development / retention, assessment of 12 DPs and 16 future GMs (regional franchise managers).	With wall charts, overall set of names is debated; players moved as appropriate; list key action items; functional names may be added by functional EC members.	90 mins.
Open GM positions and people-in-play	Identify potential slates of candidates for anticipated vacancies (next three to six months); use for future slating for vacancies.	Build flip chart over course of two days of potential openings; use list to gain nominations based on all data points from the two days.	60 mins.
Conclusions and summary actions	Summarize all key action items and set stage for next day.	Process continues day 2 with key functional roles.	15 mins.

Tool #14: Global Leadership Behaviors: Assessment

Application: Global team members complete this as a self-assessment and then ask peers to rate them as a basis for sharing feedback with each other.

1. **Feel responsible to act.** Focus on the customer, take decisions, and create results for your team and the larger team.

   Rarely   1   2   3   4   5   Nearly Always

   (continued)

2. **Take ownership.** Take accountability for your actions and behaviors, and deliver on your commitments.

   Rarely   1   2   3   4   5   Nearly Always

3. **Team up for excellence.** Break the silos and collaborate with colleagues across the customer value chain.

   Rarely   1   2   3   4   5   Nearly Always

4. **Hit the Pause Button.** Gain control over your reactive "hot button" patterns.

   Rarely   1   2   3   4   5   Nearly Always

5. **Hidden agendas.** Bring the unspoken topics into the conversation to resolve them.

   Rarely   1   2   3   4   5   Nearly Always

6. **Courageous conversations.** Frame your communication to get needs met mutually rather than a win/lose scenario.

   Rarely   1   2   3   4   5   Nearly Always

7. **Take a balcony moment.** Provide an "outside-in" perspective to get out of old patterns and try new behaviors.

   Rarely   1   2   3   4   5   Nearly Always

Tool #15: Three Matrix Leadership Roles

Application: Use in leadership workshops to introduce leaders to the three broad types of matrix leadership roles—Tiebreaker, Matrix Leader, Matrix Manager—and the success behaviors for each. Can be used as self-assessment by asking each leader to rate themselves on the behaviors associated with the role that they hold in the new organization, or can be done as a card sort, table exercise to frame a discussion on leader behaviors. (See Figure 11.2.)

(continued)

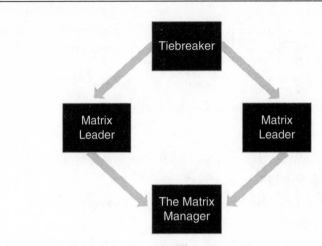

Figure 11.2   Three matrix leadership roles.

The Matrix Manager Behaviors
- Serve as an effective member of both leadership teams—advocate when necessary and take the *unpopular view* when required. Treat both sets of priorities as equally important.

- Move business information from one axis to the other— (e.g., bring the voice of the customer into franchise discussions, and bring franchise strategy voice back to the market).

- Proactively align your work agenda and priorities to support the growth strategy of the franchise in the region context.

- Ensure clarity on "who owns what" with peers and other stakeholders (e.g., balance the voice of the customer with efficiency needs).

- Actively build networks for yourself and for your team—establish real relationships and understand the interests of your partners.

(continued)

The Matrix Leader Behaviors

- Proactively engage peer leader(s) in:

  - setting and monitoring the business plan;

  - allocating resources across opportunities; and

  - all key employee life cycle events.

- Communicate the strategy and the criteria for trade-offs among options.

- Cofacilitate communications sessions to assure a single message and understanding.

- Delegate decisions down—be a role model for trust in your team and peers. *Avoid involvement in unnecessary details.*

- When there is a conflict or a choice to be made:

  - choose the best interests of the total company over your unit;

  - seek consistency when possible vs. variability that doesn't add value; and

  - escalate issues that you cannot resolve with your peer(s).

The Tiebreaker Behaviors

- Make sure that roles and metrics are clear. Be a constant coach on how to get things done in the matrix.

- Facilitate sessions to align objectives and priorities where it is important.

- Clarify decision rights. Be sure the right people are involved in the right decisions.

- Bring people physically together to build networks.

- Recognize positive efforts to make the handshake work.

- Determine when to make decisions and when to push it back down.

- Seize "teaching moments"—help others understand how decisions support the broader enterprise.

Tool #16: Delegation and Trust

Application: Use as part of a leadership workshop that challenges leaders to consider carefully what decisions or tasks they choose to get involved in with lateral peers and which should be trusted to others. (See Figure 11.3.) Ask leaders to answer the four questions then share results with colleagues.

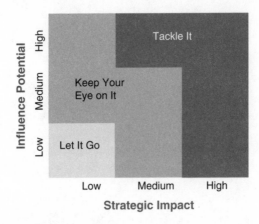

Figure 11.3   Mapping areas of concern.

Source: Susan Finerty.

1. What are a few examples of issues in the matrix that you have been involved in that you could "let go of" in the future?

2. What are a few examples of issues that you should be keeping your eye on—while being less directly involved?

3. What is an example of a "tackle-it" issue or task that you may have avoided that you should get more involved in?

4. What changes in your approach would you consider now (including delegation)?

BIBLIOGRAPHY

"GE Names Vice Chairman John Rice to Lead GE Global Growth & Operations." *BusinessWire*, November 8, 2010. www.businesswire.com/news/home/20101108006198/en/GE-Names-Vice-Chairman-John-Rice-Lead#.VWdIcGDF_ww, accessed January 14, 2015.

"Honeywell Merging Turbocharger Business into Aerospace Unit." *Automotive News*, July 2014. http://europe.autonews.com/article/20140714/OEM10/140719929/honeywell-merging-turbocharger-business-into-aerospace-unit, accessed February 21, 2015.

"Integrated Business Services: Taking Shared Services to New Heights of High Performance." Accenture Client Whitepaper, 2014.

Arons, Marc de Swaan, Frank van den Driest, and Keith Weed. "The Ultimate Marketing Machine." *Harvard Business Review*, July–August 2014 (reprint), 1–11.

Axelrod, Richard H. Axelrod, and Peter Block. *Terms of Engagement: New Ways of Leading and Changing Organizations*. Chicago: Berrett-Koehler, 2010.

Baghai, Mehrdad, Steve Coley, and David White. *The Alchemy of Growth: Practical Insights for Building the Enduring Enterprise*. New York: Basic Books, 1999.

Baghai, Mehrdad, Sven Smit, and Patrick Viguerie. "Is Your Growth Strategy Flying Blind?" *Harvard Business Review*, May 2009, 86–93.

Bennis, Warren, and Burt Nanus. *Leaders: The Strategies for Taking Charge*. New York: Harper Business, 1997.

Bennis, Warren, and Robert J. Thomas. "*Crucibles of Leadership.*" *Harvard Business Review*, September 2002. 39–47.

Bird, Allan, and Michael J. Stevens. "Assessing Global Leadership Competencies." In *Global Leadership Research, Practice, and Development, 2nd ed*, edited by Mark Mendenhall et al., 113–140. New York & London: Routledge, 2013.

Bird, Allan, and Joyce Osland. "Process Models of Global Leadership Development." In *Global Leadership Research, Practice, and Development*, 2nd ed., edited by Mark Mendenhall et al., 97–112. New York & London: Routledge, 2013.

Black, Stewart, Allan Morrison, and Hal Gregersen. *Global Explorers: The Next Generation of Leaders*. New York: Routledge, 1999.

Blodget, Henry. "Has Cisco's John Chambers Lost His Mind?" *Business Insider*, August 6, 2009. www.businessinsider.com/henry-blodget-has-ciscos-john-chambers-lost-his-mind-2009-8, accessed February 12, 2015.

Brake, Terrence. *The Global Leader: Critical Factors for Creating the World Class Organization*. New York: McGraw-Hill, 1997.

Byron, Ellen. "P&G Shakes Up Executive Ranks." *Wall Street Journal*, October 23, 2014, B1, accessed January 25, 2015.

Canning, Mike. "From Collaboration to Choreography." *Dialogue* (online journal), March 4, 2015. http://dialoguereview.com/collaboration-choreography-michael-canning/, accessed March 30, 2015.

Conaty, Bill, and Ram Charan. *The Talent Masters*. New York: Crown Publishing, 2010.

Cross, Rob, Roger Martin, and Leigh Weiss. "Mapping the Value of Employee Collaboration." *McKinsey Quarterly* (online journal), August 2006. www.mckinsey.com/insights/organization/mapping_the_value_of_employee_collaboration, accessed December 20, 2014.

DeMeuse, Kenneth, Guangrong Dai, and George Hallenbeck. "Using Learning Agility to Identify High Potentials around the World," *Korn Ferry Institute Research Study*. www.successfactors.com/static/docs/LearningAgilityResearchWhitepaper.pdf, accessed March 3, 2015.

Dodd, Dominic, and Ken Favaro. *The Three Tensions: Winning the Struggle to Perform Without Compromise*. San Francisco: Jossey-Bass, 2007.

Drotter, Stephen. *The Performance Pipeline: Getting the Right Performance at Every Level of Leadership*. San Francisco: Jossey-Bass, 2011.

Drucker, Peter. *Management*. New York: Harper & Row, 1974.

Ernst, Chris, and Donna Chrobot-Mason. *Boundary Spanning Leadership: Six Practices for Solving Problems, Driving Innovation, and Transforming Organizations*. New York: McGraw Hill, 2011.

Esterl, Mike. "At Coke, Newest Flavor is Austerity." *Wall Street Journal*, December 23, 2014. www.wsj.com/articles/at-coke-newest-flavor-is-austerity-1419352337, accessed December 23, 2014.

Few, Stephen. *Information Dashboard Design: The Effective Visual Communication of Data*. Sebastopol, CA: O'Reilly Media, 2006.

Finerty, Susan. *Master the Matrix: 7 Essentials for Getting Things Done in Complex Organizations*. Minneapolis, MN: Two Harbors Press, 2012.

Frisch, Bob. "Who Really Makes the Big Decisions in Your Company?" *Harvard Business Review*, December 2011, 52–63.

Galbraith, Jay R. *Competing with Flexible Lateral Organizations*. Boston: Addison-Wesley, 1994.

Galbraith, Jay R. "The Evolution of Enterprise Organization Designs." *Journal of Organization Design* 1 (2012): 1–13.

Galbraith, Jay R. *Designing Organizations: Strategy, Structure, and Process at the Business Unit and Enterprise Levels*. New York: Springer, 2014.

Govindarajan, Vijay, and Chris Trimble. *Reverse Innovation: Create Far from Home, Win Everywhere*. Boston: Harvard Business Press, 2012.

Heath, Chip, and Dan Heath. *Switch: How to Change Things When Change Is Hard*. New York: Crown Publishing Group, 2010.

Jaques, Elliott. *Requisite Organization: The CEO's Guide to Creative Structure and Leadership*. Greensboro: Carson-Dellosa Publishing, 1989.

Jargon, Julie. "McDonald's Plans to Change U.S. Structure." *Wall Street Journal*, October 30, 2014. www.wsj.com/articles/mcdonalds-to-change-u-s-structure-1414695278, accessed October 30, 2014.

Lafley, Alan G., and Roger L. Martin. 2013. *Playing to Win: How Strategy Really Works*. Boston: Harvard Business Review Press, 2013.

Lombardo, Michael M., and Robert W. Eichinger. *FYI: For Your Improvement*. Minneapolis, MN: Lominger Limited, 2004.

Lovallo, Dan, and Olivier Sibony. "The Case for Behavioral Strategy." *McKinsey Quarterly* (online journal), March 2010. www.mckinsey.com/insights/strategy/the_case_for_behavioral_strategy.

Kates, Amy. "Designing Organizations for Digital Success." In *Strategic Digital Marketing*, by Eric Greenberg and Alexander Kates, 283–310. New York: McGraw-Hill, 2013.

Kesler, Gregory. "How Coke's CEO Aligned Strategy and People to Re-Charge Growth: An Interview with Neville Isdell." *People and Strategy* 31 (2008): 18–21.

Kesler, Gregory. "What Business Can Learn from the Non-Profit (and Vice-Versa): An Interview with Special Olympics CEO, Tim Shriver." *People and Strategy* 34 (2011): 40-44.

Kesler, Gregory, and Amy Kates. *Leading Organization Design: How to Make Organization Design Decisions to Drive the Results You Want*. Hoboken, NJ: John Wiley & Sons, 2011.

McGuire, John B., and Gary Rhodes. *Transforming Your Leadership Culture*. Hoboken, NJ: John Wiley & Sons, 2009.

Mendenhall, Mark, Joyce Osland, Allan Bird, Gary Oddou, Martha Maznevski, Michael Stevens, and Gunter Stahl. *Global Leadership Research, Practice, and Development, 2nd ed*. New York & London: Routledge, 2013.

Mocker, M., P. Weill, and S. Woerner. "Revisiting Complexity in the Digital Age." *MIT Sloan Management Review* on-line, Summer 2014. http://sloanreview.mit.edu/article/revisiting-complexity-in-the-digital-age/.

Moorman, Christine. "Marketing in a Technology Company: GE's Organizational Platform for Innovation." *Forbes*, January 29, 2013. www.forbes.com/sites/christinemoorman/2013/01/29/marketing-in-a-technology-company-ges-organizational-platform-for-innovation/, accessed February 9, 2015.

Murray, Alan. "The End of Management." *Wall Street Journal*, August 21, 2010. www.wsj.com/articles/SB10001424052748704476104575439723695579664, accessed January 25, 2015.

Prahalad, Coimbatore K. "Globalization: The Intellectual and Managerial Challenges." *Human Resource Management* 29 (1990): 27–37.

Roberto, Michael A. *Why Great Leaders Don't Take Yes for an Answer: Managing for Conflict and Consensus*. New York: FT Press, 2013.

Schuster, Michael, and Greg Kesler. "Aligning Reward Systems in Organization Design." *People & Strategy* 34 (2011): 38–45.

Shell, G. Richard, and Mario Moussa. *The Art of Woo: Using Strategic Persuasion to Sell Your Ideas*. New York: Penguin Books, 2008.

Suchman, Anthony L. "Organizations as Machines, Organizations as Conversations: Two Core Metaphors and Their Consequences." *Medical Care* 49 (2011): S43–S48.

Sull, Donald, and Charles Spinosa. "Promise-Based Management: The Essence of Execution." *Harvard Business Review*, April 2007, 78–89.

Sull, Donald. "How to Thrive in Turbulent Markets." *Harvard Business Review*, February 2009, 54–67.

Sull, Donald, Rebecca Homkes, and Charles Sull. "Why Strategy Execution Unravels—and What to Do About It." *Harvard Business Review*, April 2015, 25–36.

Tapscott, Don, and Anthony D. Williams. *Wikinomics: How Mass Collaboration Changes Everything*. London: Portfolio, 2010.

Tichy, Noel M., Michael I. Brimm, Ram Charan, and Hirotaka Takeuchi. "Leadership Development as a Lever for Global Transformation." In *Globalizing Management, Creating and Leading the Competitive Organization*, edited by V. Pucik, N. Tichy and C.K. Barnett, 47–60. New York: John Wiley and Sons, 1992.

Viguerie, Patrick, Sven Smit, and Mehrdad Baghai. *The Granularity of Growth: How to Identify the Sources of Growth and Drive Enduring Company Performance*. Hoboken, NJ: John Wiley & Sons, 2008.

Weisbord, Marvin, and Sandra Janoff. *Future Search: Getting the Whole System in the Room for Vision, Commitment, and Action*. Chicago: Berrett-Koehler, 2010.

Zaleznick, Abraham. "Power and Politics in the Organizational Life." *Harvard Business Review*, November–December 1956, 25–29.

About the Authors

Amy Kates

Amy works with leaders and their teams to assess organizational issues, reshape structures and processes, and build depth of management capability. She is a skilled diagnostician and designer and helps her clients to understand organizational options and their implications, and to make sound decisions.

In addition to her consulting work, she teaches organization design in the Executive MBA program at the Executive School of Business in Denmark, at Ashridge Business School in the U.K., and through Cornell University. Amy is a past editor of the journal *People & Strategy*. This is Amy's fourth book on organization design. Amy has her graduate and undergraduate degrees from Cornell University.

Gregory Kesler

Greg consults with corporations in organization design and executive talent management.

He is the coauthor of *Leading Organization Design* (Jossey-Bass, 2011) as well as numerous articles and book chapters. He teaches and speaks on the subject to executive groups around the world.

Greg has led whole-company, global redesign projects and succession planning initiatives at numerous multinational companies. He specializes in designing and implementing global operating models and governance practices in large global companies.

Before beginning his consulting career, Greg held senior human resource management positions in the United States and Europe for three Fortune 200 companies. Greg holds a master's degree in organization and human relations from the University of Kansas.

INDEX

Page references followed by *fig* indicate an illustrated figure; followed by *t* indicate at table.